THE COURT-MARTIAL TRIAL OF WEST POINT CADET JOHNSON WHITTAKER

A Headline Court Case

Headline Court Cases

THE COURT-MARTIAL TRIAL OF WEST POINT CADET JOHNSON WHITTAKER

A Headline Court Case

Valerie A. Gray

Enslow Publishers, Inc.

40 Industrial Road	PO Box 38
Box 398	Aldershot
Berkeley Heights, NJ 07922	Hants GU12 6BP
USA	UK

http://www.enslow.com

Library of Congress Cataloging-in-Publication Data

Gray, Valerie A.
 The court-martial trial of West Point cadet Johnson Whittaker: a
headline court case / Valerie A. Gray.
       p. cm. — (Headline court cases)
Includes bibliographical references and index.
 ISBN 0-7660-1485-1
 1. Whittaker, Johnson Chestnut, 1858-1931—Trials, litigation,
etc.—Juvenile literature. 2. Courts-martial and courts of inquiry—New
York (State)—Juvenile literature. 3. Race discrimination—New York
(State)—History—Juvenile literature. 4. Military cadets—New York
(State)—History—Juvenile literature. [1. Whittaker, Johnson Chestnut,
1858-1931—Trials, litigation, etc. 2. Courts-martial and courts of
inquiry—New York (State) 3. Race discrimination. 4. Military
cadets—History. 5. Trials.] I. Title. II. Series.
 KF7642.W47 G73   2001
 343.73'0143—dc21   00-012169

Printed in the United States of America

10 9 8 7 6 5 4 3 2 1

To Our Readers:
We have done our best to make sure all Internet addresses in this book were active and
appropriate when we went to press. However, the author and the publisher have no control
over and assume no liability for the material available on those Internet sites or on other
Web sites they may link to. Any comments or suggestions can be sent by e-mail to
comments@enslow.com or to the address on the back cover.

Photo Credits: © Collection of the New-York Historical Society, negative
number 73853, p. 8; © Collection of the New-York Historical Society, negative
number 73854, p. 27; Courtesy of Library of Congress, pp. 13, 17, 22, 24, 83;
Courtesy of Library of Congress, *Dictionary of American Portraits*, Dover
Publications, 1967, p. 87; Courtesy of National Archives, pp. 33, 43, 48, 53, 56,
59, 62, 67, 74, 91, 96; Courtesy of New-York Historical Society, *Dictionary of
American Portraits*, Dover Publications, 1967, p. 77; Courtesy of Ulysses
Whittaker Boykin, pp. 3, 37; Engraving by H. B. Hall's Sons, *Dictionary of
American Portraits*, Dover Publications, 1967, p. 19; From the South Carolina
Historical Society Collections, p. 71; Harper's Weekly/Library of Congress,
p. 45; South Carolina State University Historical Collection, pp. 79, 81.

Cover Photo: South Carolina State University Historical Collection (color
portrait); National Archives (background).

Contents

chapter one

THE ATTACK

WEST POINT—Johnson Chestnut Whittaker was the only African-American cadet at West Point in 1880. He was a "trailblazer" in the new process of introducing black cadets into the all-white United States Military Academy. The Civil War had ended slavery, but it had not ended the cultural hatred of African Americans that still existed throughout the country. During his four years at West Point, Whittaker was ignored and considered an outcast by the white cadets. He endured racial slurs and physical attacks. But the abuse that he suffered got even worse on April 6, 1880, when, in the middle of the night, Whittaker was brutally beaten in his room.

Three masked attackers entered Whittaker's room. He was awakened when one of the attackers jumped on his bed. Whittaker was startled as he tried to struggle with his attacker. Whittaker was punched in the nose. One attacker said, "Let us shave his head." Another said, "Let us mark him as we mark hogs down South."[1] To follow through on their threats, the attackers forced Whittaker to the floor and tied his feet together. As one attacker raised a knife, Whittaker put up his hands to protect his face. Instead of cutting his face, the attackers cut Whittaker's left hand and ear. One of the attackers said, "Let me put my handkerchief under his ear so that he won't bleed too much."[2] They also cut patches of his hair.

In an effort to humiliate Whittaker further, one attacker put a mirror to his face so that he could see what had been done to him. After Whittaker saw himself, one attacker struck him with the mirror, breaking the glass. Then the

© Collection of the New-York Historical Society, negative number 73853

At the time of the attack, Johnson Whittaker was the only African-American cadet at West Point.

attackers tied Whittaker's feet to the frame of the bed and tied his wrists together. The last words that Whittaker heard from his attackers were, "Then he will leave."[3] With these words, the attackers revealed their motive for scaring Whittaker. They wanted the only African-American cadet to leave West Point.

Whittaker's mistreatment did not end there, though. Actually, the attack was just the beginning. Suffering from his injuries was not enough. After investigating the attack, officials at West Point concluded that Whittaker had staged the entire thing and inflicted the injuries on himself.

Whittaker's story illustrates the conditions in the United States in the late 1800s that made overt racism—obvious and outwardly displayed—against African Americans acceptable. Those conditions include the social and economic status of African Americans in the United States before, during, and after the Civil War and the treatment of African Americans in the United States and at West Point.

chapter two

RACISM IN THE MAKING

POST CIVIL WAR—To understand how Cadet Johnson Chestnut Whittaker could have been accused of staging the attack, it is important to understand the social and economic conditions that existed during this time in the United States.

History of Slavery

The institution of slavery was based on one individual owning and controlling all aspects of a black person's life. A slave did not volunteer to live this way. Ownership came from the capture or purchase of people who had been forcibly brought to the United States from Africa. The owners considered slaves to be inferior solely because of the color of their skin.

Slavery began throughout what is now the United States in the 1600s. This was when the first slaves were forcibly brought here from Africa. Slavery eventually concentrated in the South largely because of its profitability there. Slavery was important not simply for the cultivation of rice, but also for other cash crops such as tobacco, indigo, and cotton. Many slaves were brought to Maryland and Virginia. However, slavery existed throughout the United States (even in the North).

America was developing into a nation and workers were needed to help build the country. So, from the early stages of American history, slaves were used. Early slaves were known as indentured servants. This meant that they were bound by an agreement with their owners to work for them for a certain amount of time until they "earned" their freedom. After that time was up, the indentured servants could then regain their freedom. Some indentured servants had the freedom to leave the premises of their owner, but this freedom would soon change, and many indentured servants never gained that freedom.

In Virginia, indentured servants who were lucky enough to earn their freedom began to compete with whites for land ownership. Many whites did not want blacks to have the same opportunities they had; whites wanted total control of land. White landowners also decided that having a permanent black workforce would help to control the land and the slaves. To accomplish this, more blacks were brought in from Africa as slaves. The few freedoms that indentured servants had, quickly disappeared.

Many whites came to justify slavery as an act of benevolence and Christian mercy. Southern whites argued that slavery elevated the slaves to civilization and offered them exposure to Christianity. To many whites, slavery was justified as a biblical concept.

During the late 1600s, slavery expanded in South Carolina. Slave labor in South Carolina was used mainly to harvest rice. The slave owners knew that blacks in Africa were expert rice growers; they also knew that growing rice was very hard work. So, more and more blacks were taken from Africa to work in the states. By 1720, the black population in South Carolina was almost double that of the white population. Whites became fearful that blacks might try to revolt to end slavery.[1] This fear led to laws that further limited the few freedoms that the slaves had. The Negro Act of 1740 took away all rights and freedoms from slaves. The act allowed slave owners to enforce stricter punishment on slaves who disobeyed.

To escape the worsening conditions, many African Americans fought in the Revolutionary War (1775–1783), America's fight to gain its independence from Great Britain. Approximately fifty thousand African Americans left America to return to England with British forces.[2]

Life of a Slave

Slaves in the South worked mainly in three locations: on small farms, on large plantations, and in the plantation houses. Farms and plantations were distinguished by the size of the property, both in land and number of slaves. (Plantations had more of both.) The conditions were different at each location but slaves were always forced to work hard. Farm slaves worked the land on small farms. Their owners usually would supervise them directly. Plantation slaves worked on large farms as field hands.

Plantations had overseers. The overseer was responsible for making sure the crops were picked, the slaves were obedient, and the plantation was running efficiently. The overseer was unpopular with slaves. He would bark orders and punish slaves if he felt they were not working hard enough. If slaves tried to escape, the overseer would hunt them down. Punishment was given in front of all other slaves to make sure that everyone understood what would happen if they tried to escape or disobey. Punishment could come in the form of a beating with a whip. The success of the farm or plantation depended on slave labor.

House slaves were usually female. They would clean the plantation house and prepare meals. Slaves also worked as gardeners, blacksmiths, and carpenters.

Of course, during this time there was no farm machinery like tractors. Slaves had to till the soil with a hoe or pick cotton by hand. The heat and humidity in the South can be intense. Slaves had to work many hours under the sun with few breaks. Their only day off was Sunday. During harvest time, when the crops were

The life of a slave was never easy. Here a family is torn apart as only the husband is sold to that particular owner.

picked, every slave—young or old, male or female—was expected to work long, grueling hours in the fields.

Slave owners, like all people, had different personalities and treated their slaves differently. To reward slaves for their hard work, some owners would give their slaves a garden plot, days off, or permission to leave the plantation for a brief period of time.

A typical day for slave children did not include going to school. In the 1820s and 1830s laws were passed to make it illegal for a slave to be educated. An educated slave was a powerful slave. Slave owners believed that education could lead to slaves getting together to plan an escape. Owners also believed that if educated, slaves would read abolitionist literature that would lead them to turn against their owners and start a revolt. Abolitionists were people who wanted slavery to end. Their literature focused on why slavery was wrong. Slave owners believed blacks were inferior. They did not want to waste time teaching slaves to read and write when all they were ever going to be was field workers. However, there were a few owners who allowed some of their slaves to learn how to read and write. Those owners were never punished for disobeying the law; but slaves who were caught reading or writing were punished.

Slaves tried to make the best of their situation by establishing communities on the plantations. They held church services, wedding ceremonies, social gatherings, and told stories. Although the wedding ceremonies were considered legal in the eyes of the slave couple, it was illegal for slaves to marry according to the laws of the United

States at that time. There were also networks of slave communities to alert others of escape plans. This was done secretly through messages, songs, or even patterns on quilts that were displayed on fences.

Slaves lived insecure lives. They were uncertain whether family members would be sold to other owners, breaking up the family. Many slave owners believed that their behavior toward slaves was acceptable. They actually believed that slaves thought it was honorable for them to be submissive and that it was the slave's choice to be a slave. "She waits on me because she so pleases. . . ." "We are good to our slaves." "She chooses to wait on us," some owners were heard to declare.[3]

Moving Closer to a Civil War

In 1840, the states that had slaves were Alabama, Arkansas, Delaware, Georgia, Florida, Kentucky, Louisiana, Maryland, Mississippi, Missouri, North Carolina, South Carolina, Tennessee, and Virginia. These states relied heavily on the labor of slaves for picking cotton, rice, and tobacco. In the 1840s and 1850s, the economic growth of the United States increased rapidly. In the slave states there were 4 million slaves out of a total population of 12 million people.

The United States was basically divided into two sections: the North and the South. Although it was one country, each section operated separately. The division affected politics and how the majority voted on important issues. Many Northerners were Republicans; many

Southerners were Democrats. The approach to economics and social change was different among Republicans and Democrats. Many Democrats believed in the idea of states' rights, meaning that each state should make its own laws. Many Republicans supported a national concept of laws and hoped to abolish slavery.

Economic growth in the North came largely from the building of railways and factories. The North demonstrated that money could be made without the use of slave labor. Many African Americans and immigrants went to Northern states seeking employment. This helped to increase the population in the North and created more urban centers and banks. The dream of freedom and opportunity tempted many slaves to escape and go to the North.

However, the slave trade and slave labor was so profitable that white Southerners were richer than white Northerners. The cost to maintain slaves was minimal and slaves were not paid a salary for their work. Their houses consisted of one-room shacks on the plantations or a room in the back of the plantation house. Southern slave owners made every effort to justify slavery to Northern citizens. However, their justification was based solely on racist thoughts and attitudes. Some scholars said that blacks lacked motivation to work and that they had an abnormal mental condition that led them to run away. Of course, they wanted to run away—they had been forcibly brought to America, held against their will, and forced to work long, strenuous hours. Others claimed that stripping Africans of their native culture and identity made them civilized. Racist thoughts like these helped to keep slavery in existence.

People in both the North and the South feared the corruption of their liberties and the corruption of the purity of their government. Each side came to see the other as a threat to liberty.

Northerners feared that supporters of slavery were conspiring to control the government and to spread the evils of slavery across the country. Some opposed slavery on

This illustration depicting a slave state on the left side of the picture and a free state on the right side brings to life the raging conflict that the issue of slavery presented.

moral grounds, but many opposed slavery because they feared competition with blacks.

Southerners also feared a loss of liberty. They saw Lincoln and his Republican Party as people whose only goal was to deny them the right to own slaves. They preferred to tear the country apart rather than wait for Lincoln and his abolitionist followers to tear down slavery—something they considered a legacy of the Founding Fathers. So the Civil War between the North and the South began when the two sides could not settle their disagreements over slavery.

The Civil War (1861–1865) was the bloodiest war in American history. It pitted Northern Americans against Southern Americans. Northerners fought in the Union Army; Southerners fought in the Confederate Army.

On July 17, 1862, Congress passed the Second Confiscation and Militia Act, freeing slaves who had owners in the Confederate Army. This way more blacks could fight in the war. As more soldiers were needed, more black men were recruited. Although blacks fought for both sides, their acceptance was not immediate and their ability to fight was questioned.

Even though this was not the first war that blacks fought in for America, the white soldiers on both sides had never fought beside blacks. So black regiments or military units were formed. The Special Colored Troops Division of the War Department was organized to recruit black soldiers in 1863. Ten percent of soldiers in the Union Army were black. The Confederate Army also organized black regiments. Many times, soldiers in the black Confederate regiments faced moral dilemmas because they were fighting to keep slavery alive. But many of them fought for the Confederate Army because they felt they did not have a choice.

On January 1, 1863, President Abraham Lincoln issued the Emancipation Proclamation. When the Civil War began, Northerners saw the war as a way to crush the rebellion and reunite the states. But Abraham Lincoln and those who saw slavery as evil seized the opportunity to make the war a battle for freedom. Southerners would have to pay a price for the rebellion—they would lose their slaves if they were defeated. Although the Emancipation Proclamation did not actually free any slaves, on January 1, 1863, wherever Union troops went, they became armies of freedom.

Battles were fought in Northern and Southern states. Both sides experienced victories and defeats. More and more, the Union Army won the battles and those areas of the South came under Union control. Four years after the Civil War began, the Union Army had control over all Southern states. The North was victorious and the Civil

President Abraham Lincoln is credited with issuing the Emancipation Proclamation in 1863, and helping to free the slaves.

War ended. Slavery was abolished throughout the United States.

The End of Slavery and the Civil War

The end of the Civil War led to chaos for many. Expectations among free African Americans were high. They wanted equal treatment. But slavery and racism were deeply rooted in the thinking of many people. Slaves expected the war to bring them political freedom along with the opportunity to own land and receive an education.[4] Unfortunately, African Americans were still in the same economic and educational condition after the war that they had been in during slavery.

Reconstruction

Reconstruction was the period between 1865 and 1877 when Southern states were reorganized to again become part of the United States. Southerners had lost the war, but they showed little remorse. President Lincoln's assassination by a Confederate sympathizer only made Northerners more anxious to punish the South. Southerners were forced to accept the fact that African Americans had rights, and to allow them to vote and hold public office. Despite the presence of Union armies throughout the South, Southerners fought to maintain the social order that put African Americans at the bottom.

Eventually, Northerners grew tired of enforcing the new social order in the South. They became absorbed in their own political and economic problems. In 1877 a deal was made and Southerners regained control of their own affairs—with disastrous results for African Americans' hopes for equality and freedom.

Northern sympathy for African Americans as human beings and a desire to elevate them to a higher level of social equality was limited. Although the Civil War had ended slavery, it had not abolished the deep-rooted racism in both the North and South.

Since slaves were not educated, most were illiterate. Only 10 percent of African Americans could read and write.[5] It took time for former slaves to adjust to their freedom.

After slavery many African Americans traveled long distances looking for loved ones who had been traded to other owners. Others wanted to make their marriages legal since slave marriages were not recognized. Parents also protected

During the early years of Reconstruction, many former slaves settled together in freedmen's villages, like this one in Arlington, Virginia. They wanted to get away from the plantations that had enslaved them.

their children from the uncertainties that the future held. One way this was accomplished was through the establishment of communities. These communities served as an extended family for the children, which led to a sense of security for the African-American children. Religion also helped with the adjustment.

African Americans wanted the American dream: freedom, family, education, and land. This dream would not come easily, however. As they made strides toward making the dream come true, they were met with resistance. But a select few were able to overcome great odds.

As part of the Reconstruction, blacks were given some of the same freedoms and rights as whites. They could vote and hold offices such as police, justices of the peace, and even Justices of the Supreme Court. Jonathan Jasper Wright, an African American, was an Associate Justice of the Supreme Court of South Carolina from 1870 until 1877. Twenty-eight African Americans were senators and representatives in Alabama, Georgia, Florida, Louisiana, Mississippi, North Carolina, and South Carolina.

Johnson Chestnut Whittaker's education came at the height of the Reconstruction period.

chapter three

SETTING THE STAGE

HOME LIFE—Johnson Chestnut Whittaker and his twin brother, Jeems, were born into slavery on August 23, 1858, on the Mulberry plantation near Camden, South Carolina. When Johnson and Jeems were born, their father, James, had purchased his freedom and was a free man. Their mother, Maria, was still a slave. Johnson also had another brother who was two years older. Maria Whittaker was the personal maid of plantation owner Mary Boykin Chestnut.

Mary Chestnut was a Civil War diarist. She wrote briefly about the Whittakers. According to her, "she [Maria] is left forlorn for the sad and involuntary crime of twins."[1] The "crime" that she was referring to was James' reaction to the birth of the twins. James did not recognize the twins as his sons. This was the first time twins had been born in his family, and he did not think Johnson and Jeems could be his sons. James left the family shortly after the twins were born. Maria and her sons remained on the Mulberry plantation as slaves.

As the personal maid to Mary Boykin Chestnut, Maria Whittaker lived in the main house on the Mulberry plantation. Although the living conditions were somewhat better for house slaves than for field slaves, Maria Whittaker's duties were many; and she was not free. She was told what to do, how to do it, and when to do it. She was responsible for domestic duties, including cooking, washing, cleaning, and seeing to Mary Boykin Chestnut's personal needs such as dressing and bathing her and combing her hair.

Even before Johnson and Jeems were seven years old, they had responsibilities as slaves. Slave children had to

Johnson Chestnut Whittaker and his twin brother, Jeems, were born into slavery on August 23, 1858, on the Mulberry plantation near Camden, South Carolina. The main house on the plantation is shown here.

work in the fields picking cotton and keeping the soil free of weeds. They also had to help clean the inside and outside of the plantation house.

After the Civil War, Johnson, his mother, and his brothers moved to Camden, South Carolina, where Maria Whittaker worked as a maid. Johnson and his brothers attended a freedman's school, a school set up to educate former slaves. At the age of twelve, Johnson was tutored by a black minister in the Camden area. During this time, he also worked as a bricklayer's assistant. The Whittaker family was saddened when Jeems died in an accident at the age of thirteen.

In 1874, Johnson, then just sixteen, entered the University of South Carolina in Columbia, South Carolina. During Reconstruction, the University of South Carolina was integrated. Black students could attend the college together with white students. This was quite a change for the white students and faculty. Many let their racist attitudes get in the way of receiving an education. The change was so difficult for the majority of students and faculty that many white students stopped attending and many white teachers quit teaching.[2] Teachers from Northern states were hired as replacements. African-American enrollment at the university grew. Tuition for the students was paid through endowments, gifts of money, that were provided by wealthy Northern and Southern businessmen. Southern states also provided grants, money given to students by the government, for tuition.

During his time at college, Whittaker changed the

spelling of his name. As a slave, Johnson's father had been given his owner's last name. The Whitaker family spelled its name with one "t." While at college, Johnson added another "t" to his last name, making the spelling "Whittaker." Perhaps he added the second "t" to separate himself from slavery and his former owners.

Johnson excelled academically during his first two years at the University of South Carolina, and one of his professors, Richard Greener, recommended him as a candidate for appointment to West Point Military Academy.

Professor Greener was well respected and had very impressive credentials. In 1870, he became the first African American to graduate from Harvard University. On the nomination of South Carolina Republican congressman S. L. Hoge, Johnson Chestnut Whittaker entered West Point in 1876. Because the process was relatively private, Whittaker did not meet much opposition to being nominated. There was no big announcement of his arrival at West Point. However, once Whittaker arrived, he was not welcomed at West Point with open arms.

History of West Point

West Point Military Academy is an institution that trains and educates students for service in the United States Army. The academy is located in West Point, New York, along the Hudson River approximately fifty miles north of New York City. Currently, the academy sits on sixteen thousand acres of land. After graduating from West Point, cadets receive a Bachelor of Science degree and a commission, which means they are appointed as a second lieutenant in the Army. The United States government bought the academy in 1790. On March 16, 1802, Congress passed an act to establish the United States Military Academy at West Point. It opened in this capacity on July 4, 1802. During this time, the academy served as an apprentice school, a school that teaches a skill, for military engineers. Later, it served as the first school of engineering in the United States.

The purpose of the academy in its early days was to train military technicians, people who understood how the machinery used in the military worked, and to encourage the study of military topics and the sciences.[3] On April 29, 1812, the academy was recognized by Congress as a four-year college. Very slowly, the academy began to resemble a

© Collection of the New-York Historical Society, negative number 73854

The building that serves as a dormitory for cadets at West Point was built in 1815.

college campus. The barracks, a dormitory, was built in 1815. The barracks did not have running water and the cadets slept on blankets on the floor. In fact, the academy did not have beds or running water until the 1840s.

The superintendent of West Point in 1817 was Sylvanus Thayer. A superintendent is the person in charge of making decisions about how the school is run. He organized the courses of study that are still followed today. The courses are more focused today than before, however. Cadets today take classes in such subjects as mathematics, engineering, science, military science, physical education, and philosophy.[4] Beginning in 1843, cadets had to be appointed—or nominated—by a member of Congress or the president of the United States in order to get into the academy.

A cadet's life at West Point was very orderly. Actually, every aspect of the cadets' living conditions was controlled. There were instructions for the cadets on how to clean and maintain the appearance of their rooms. The instructions were called Special Regulations for Barracks. The instructions were posted on the door of each room. If a cadet did not keep his room orderly, he would be given demerits. A demerit is a mark recorded against him for a fault in behavior or appearance.

Each cadet had to be in full dress from 8 A.M. to 10 A.M. for inspection. Full dress consisted of a uniform coat that always had to be buttoned, gloves, and side arms (weapons). A cadet's shoes always had to be clean and free of dust.

All of the cadet's equipment had to be stored in a

specific location. For example, waist belts and swords had to be hung on pegs near the gun-rack shelf. There were even rules for bedding. The mattress had to be folded once. The blankets and comforter had to be folded neatly and the folds could not be wider than the pillow.

Cadets during this time did not have modern conveniences. The spittoon, a bucket to spit into while brushing teeth, had to be kept near the mantelpiece. The slop bucket, which was used as a toilet, had to be kept next to the wash stand.[5]

These regulations not only made sure that each barrack was clean, they also instilled discipline and order in the lives of cadets. All cadets were "on the same page"—thinking alike and knowing what to expect. This was important, particularly for a military institution, because when everyone has the same training, the likelihood of disagreement decreases. The atmosphere tends to be more like a family and bonds are strong. One big disadvantage to this system is that one change can upset everyone involved and can lead to persecution. In this case, change led to racial persecution against the first African Americans to enter West Point.

African Americans at West Point

With the end of slavery in 1865, African Americans were considered citizens according to the Constitution, even though society in general did not recognize their equal rights. Government officials were interested in the equal rights of African Americans for political as well as moral reasons. West Point was one of the first government institutions to include African-American cadets. Benjamin F. Butler, a former Union general and congressman from Massachusetts, was the first person to discuss appointing an African American to West Point.[6] He knew that the first African-American cadet had to be able to take the social and academic pressures that would surely come.

When a person paves the way for others, he or she must possess certain characteristics. A strong character and the ability to handle difficult situations and withstand harsh treatment are important factors. Friends and any type of a social life will not exist. That was the case for African-American cadets. Since the racist attitude that blacks were inferior prevailed in American society, it would be hard for white cadets to think of them as their equals. Five years after the Civil War, these feelings were still strong. So with politicians, citizens, and newspapers following the story, West Point set out to enroll its first African-American cadet.

South Carolina congressman Solomon L. Hoge nominated African American James Smith for appointment to West Point. At the time of the appointment, Smith was attending Howard University in Washington, D.C. However, before Smith could enroll at West Point he had to pass the academy's difficult physical and mental examinations. Smith was the only African American, out of a total of thirty-seven people, to pass the exam.[7] He walked through the halls of West Point on May 31, 1879. Within hours of arriving he was bombarded with racial slurs. The attitudes toward Smith were formed before the cadets had a chance to get to know him. Their attitudes were based totally on his race. Said Smith of his treatment,

> I had to take every insult that was offered, without saying anything, for I had complained several times to the commandment of cadets and after investigating the matter he invariably came to the conclusion "from the evidence deduced" that I was in the wrong. . . .[8]

Smith believed that he had every right to be treated like every other cadet. He wanted the abuse to stop, so he decided to make his complaints public. He wrote of his treatment to his sponsor, David Clark. As a sponsor, Clark provided financial support and looked out for Smith's best interests by making sure he was treated fairly. Clark sent the complaints to newspapers. Congressmen were also notified of his treatment, and they went to West Point to investigate the complaints. The congressmen held hearings and concluded that Smith had, indeed, been harassed. They recommended a court-martial, a court of military officers who are appointed by a commander to try military personnel in a military court for offenses committed under military law. The officers decide if military law has been violated. Instead of agreeing with the congressmen, Secretary of War William W. Belknap issued reprimands to the cadets involved.[9]

Smith followed the proper channels of command in an attempt to stop the abuse. But he also broke the code of conduct among cadets—he "told" on his fellow cadets.

Smith's treatment affected his studies. He had to repeat his first year. The *New York Daily Graphic* newspaper published an article describing Smith's life at West Point. Regarding his decline in his studies, Smith stated, "If there is an obscure point in my lesson I must go to the class with it. I cannot go to a brother cadet."[10] When asked what would be the response of a cadet, Smith said, "They would call me a [n———] and tell me to go back to the plantation."[11]

The reprimands issued to the cadets did not lead to a decrease in their harassment of Smith. Fed up with the abuse, Smith decided to take matters into his own hands. After a fellow cadet insulted him, a fight started. Both received three weeks' confinement. They had to stay in certain areas, and they had to perform extra duties.

Cadets at the academy were convinced that Smith was "pushing too hard" for social equality and was "less concerned with receiving a military education" than with the racial equality issue.[12] He held on academically and socially for three more years; however, in June 1874, he failed natural and experimental philosophy and he was dismissed from the academy. He returned to South Carolina where he became a mathematics teacher at South Carolina Agriculture and Mechanics Institute.

Henry Ossian Flipper was the second African-American cadet to enter West Point. He was born in Thomasville, Georgia, on March 21, 1856. Flipper was born into slavery. Rueben H. Lucky, a Methodist minister, owned him and his mother, Isabella. His father, Festus, worked as a shoemaker. Festus was separated from the family because another family bought him. Festus wanted to reunite his family, so with the assistance of his owner, Ephraim Ponder, a slave dealer,

Henry Ossian Flipper was the second African-American cadet to enter West Point in 1873.

Festus was able to buy his own wife and child.[13] They were all slaves, but the family was together. In 1859, the Flippers moved to Atlanta, Georgia, with their owners. The family grew to include four more sons.

Henry was luckier than many other slaves. Mrs. Ponder gave permission for him to receive an education on the plantation, even though this was illegal for slaves.

With the end of slavery, Flipper had the opportunity to attend college. When Flipper was a first-year student at Atlanta University, Georgia congressman James Freeman appointed him to the United States Military Academy. On July 1, 1873, Flipper became a cadet. Until Smith left the academy, he and Flipper roomed together.

Flipper's first month was different from Smith's. Flipper was met with greetings and kind words. But things soon changed. Cadet Flipper said,

> When I was a [first-year student] those of us who lived on the same floor of barracks visited each other, borrowed books, heard each other recite when preparing for examinations, and were really on most intimate terms. But alas! in

less than a month they learned to call me [n——] and ceased altogether to visit me.[14]

Although he could not prove it, Flipper attributed the change in treatment to the biased comments and advice that those in his class were receiving from older cadets and family and friends. From this point, Cadet Flipper described his four years at West Point as "years of patient endurance and hard and persistent work . . . as well as weary barren wastes of loneliness, isolation, unhappiness, and melancholy."[15] The only times Flipper could escape isolation would be when he visited the barbershop or cafeteria—both places had African-American workers he could talk to. One positive note was that Flipper reported his teachers treated him fairly.

African-American newspapers at this time reported the black perspective on different issues. Several of these newspapers reported on the treatment of black cadets at West Point. *The New National Era and Citizen* reported on Flipper's isolation. But the paper also questioned the character of the white cadets and the job West Point officials were doing heading off racism against the only African-American cadet. One article said that West Point was training the white cadets to be selfish and snobbish; they did not have the discipline and integrity to not let racist acts get in the way of them being good soldiers. After all, black or white, all were West Point cadets.

Despite his isolation and the acts of hostility toward him, Cadet Flipper graduated on June 14, 1877. He ranked fiftieth out of seventy-six cadets. After graduation, Flipper was promoted to Second Lieutenant in the Army, Tenth United States Cavalry.

African-American cadets were a source of pride for their community. Cadet Flipper described an incident that illustrates this fact. While taking a walk, he saw an African-American man who had served in the Union Army. The man had lost his leg while fighting during the Civil War. When they came face to face, the man saluted Cadet Flipper. Flipper returned the salute. Said the man, "That's right! That's right! Makes me glad to see it."[16] Flipper was equally proud of the former soldier. Even though Flipper had to withstand racism and isolation, this man had sacrificed a leg so that Flipper and all African Americans could have a better life.

Although Flipper did not complain about his treatment by white cadets at West Point, it was unlikely that officials at West Point were unaware of his isolation. Officials at West Point did nothing to make life easier for the African-American cadets. Their attitude was that it was up to the African-American cadets to live with prejudice and to make the best of their situation. With this attitude, it was not surprising that academy officials were upset about other African Americans entering West Point.

Between 1873 and 1875 two other African-American cadets entered West Point. They were John W. Williams and Charles A. Minnie. Both cadets roomed with Cadet Flipper because no white cadet would room with an African-American cadet. Unfortunately, Williams and Minnie were dismissed when they did not do well in their classes.

Johnson Chestnut Whittaker arrived at West Point in 1876. During his last year at West Point, Flipper roomed with Cadet Whittaker. Flipper shared his experiences with Whittaker. Both believed in nonviolence and not confronting individuals. However, from the beginning, Cadet Whittaker let it be known that he would not tolerate unjust treatment.

Cadet Whittaker's problems began one month after entering West Point. John C. McDonald, a cadet from Alabama, accused Whittaker of looking him in the eyes while passing him. To Cadet McDonald, this was a crime because he believed African Americans were inferior and that they should be submissive. During slavery, blacks could not look directly at whites because doing so showed that blacks were equal to whites. By today's standards, the idea that a black person could not look a white person directly in the eyes may seem absurd. But in 1876 this was the usual way of thinking. For looking him in the eyes, Cadet McDonald struck Whittaker in the face. Whittaker reported the incident to the cadet officer of the day. Cadet McDonald was later arrested, court-martialed, found guilty, and suspended for six months. By reporting the incident, Cadet Whittaker established that he expected to be treated equally. However, the treatment that Whittaker received in his first month at West Point would continue to worsen.

As the years passed, Whittaker would be an outcast, excluded from campus life. Basically, the only time Whittaker was spoken to was when the other cadets where shouting orders at him. Whittaker's only true friend was his Bible. It served as a source of inspiration and a friend to talk to. Whenever he was treated badly, he would turn to his Bible for inspiration and encouragement. He wrote various types of sentiments in it, such as quotations and rules and principles of life. He also marked different passages in his Bible. Some encouraging words that he wrote included:

"Try never to injure another by word, by act, or by look even."

"Forgive as soon as you are injured, and forget as soon as you forgive."

As his years at West Point continued, Cadet Johnson Whittaker became an outcast, excluded from campus life.

"Never to commit an act at which my kind mother would have to blush."

"To do right at all times, under whatever circumstances and at whatever cost."[17]

In spite of his treatment, Whittaker was able to successfully complete his first two years at West Point. His success would change during his last two years, however. Whittaker failed natural and experimental philosophy in a semiannual oral examination in January 1879. This subject dealt with how thinking relates to one's character and morals. This failure caused him to repeat his second year. Whittaker contended that his poor grade was due to the treatment and grading of his teacher and his outcast status. In his journal he wrote, "Everybody and thing seems against me this year and I am afraid they will after all [get rid of me] like poor Smith. My lot is indeed hard. Everybody frown[s] at me and long[s] to see me fall, and all because I'm a Negro."[18] Whittaker's reference to Smith was because both of them had the same philosophy teacher and both failed the class; also both complained about their treatment. Whittaker also displayed his determination, "I shall study until one or two o'clock and hereafter try to do better even under my harsh, prejudice instructors. I may yet go through if they give me half a chance."[19]

chapter four

THE INVESTIGATION

WEST POINT—On April 5, 1880, Cadet Johnson Whittaker returned to his room after eating supper. Placed on his chair in a small sealed envelope was the following note:

> Mr. Whittaker, you will be "fixed." Better keep awake. —A friend.[1]

Whittaker wondered what the note meant. He asked African-American custodian Louis Simpson what he thought of the note. Simpson told Whittaker not to worry about it. Whittaker wrote a letter to his mother that night and mentioned the note to her. He also mentioned that he would tell Superintendent General John M. Schofield about the note, but he did not.[2]

On April 7, 1880, Cadet Johnson Whittaker did not show up at reveille. Reveille is a signal given in the morning to awaken soldiers and call them to order for roll call. Usually the signal comes in the form of a soldier blowing a horn or bugle. The cadet officer of the day, George R. Burnett, went to Whittaker's barracks. As cadet officer of the day, it was Burnett's job to make sure that all cadets were in line and ready for command. Cadet Burnett knocked on the door. When Whittaker did not respond, Cadet Burnett opened the door. He saw Whittaker's ankles tied to the bed rail, his body was on the floor, his ear was slashed; chunks of hair were cut out. He had cuts on his arms and legs. There was blood on the floor, wall, and mattress. Scattered throughout his room were pieces of a smashed mirror, Whittaker's clumps of hair, burnt pieces of paper, an Indian club, and a handkerchief covered with blood. Cadet Burnett called the post surgeon, Dr. Major Charles T. Alexander. Dr. Alexander checked Whittaker's pulse and temperature and reported them normal. However, the doctor was not able to awaken Whittaker. He was unconscious. Lieutenant Colonel Henry M. Lazelle arrived; he was the officer in charge of cadets. He made sure that all cadets followed the rules. Several cadets gathered outside Whittaker's room. Both Colonel Lazelle and Dr. Alexander tried to awaken Whittaker. Whittaker's first words after waking up were, "Oh, don't cut me, I never hurt you." But even injured, Whittaker was not treated with compassion. Said Colonel Lazelle, "Get up and be a man," and Dr. Alexander pinched and shook Whittaker to consciousness.[3]

Whittaker was treated for the wounds to his ear, hand, and feet; however, he was never examined for other injuries. For example, he was not checked for internal injuries or the seriousness of the concussion (a head injury).

Cadet Whittaker was very upset about the attack. He was

alone and could not confide in anyone at West Point. He wrote a letter to his mother and to a friend, Moses P. Wester, expressing his feelings about the attack. In the letter to Wester on Wednesday, April 7, 1880, Whittaker expressed his sadness and anger. He described the attack as a "cruel barbarous outrage" that was committed only because he was African-American.[4] But, he still could not understand why someone would injure him, especially when he never injured anyone with words or his actions. Whittaker wrote that even though his injuries were not serious, they would stay with him forever.

Shortly after Whittaker completed the letter to Wester he wrote a letter to his mother. He wanted to be the first person to notify her of the attack so that he could try to ease her fears.

In both letters Whittaker expressed his confidence that West Point officers would find and punish his attackers. Little did he know the investigation would focus on him.

On the afternoon of April 7, 1880, Cadet Whittaker was questioned about the attack. Do you know who did it? Did you see their faces? Do you know of anyone who would want to harm you? Cadet Whittaker answered no to these questions.

The Commander of Cadets, Lieutenant Colonel M. M. Sorvelle, also questioned the cadets in the corps about the attack. Do you know anything about the attack on Cadet Whittaker? Do you know anything about the warning note? Every cadet answered no to these questions. Based on the answers that he received from the cadets, Lieutenant Colonel Sorvelle wrote the following:

> I do not believe it possible that three cadets can be found in the Corps who would so utterly falsify as they must have done in the total denial of all knowledge of the outrage on Cadet Whittaker, had they taken part in it; prompted to such a thing, as they must have been if at all, by the spirit of mere mischief.
>
> And it is utterly [unbelievable] that an attack, totally without apparent motive, should have been made by citizens, that for many reasons which follow, I am compelled to the belief that Cadet Whittaker has himself inflicted or consented to the infliction of all his apparent injuries; and himself arranged all the striking surrounds of his position when found at reveille on the morning of the 6th.
>
> I respectfully recommend that Cadet Whittaker be given the choice of resignation, or asking for a court of inquiry, or of a court-martial.[5]

Based on the testimony of Cadet Whittaker, the cadets in corps, Lieutenant Colonel Sorvelle, and Dr. Alexander, Lieutenant Lazelle concluded that Cadet Whittaker had inflicted the injuries on himself and staged the entire attack. In addition to believing that the other cadets could not possibly have caused such injury to Whittaker, other reasons cited were: his superficial wounds, his head injury was not severe—he was able to revive himself quickly; and he was tied with "flimsy material."[6] The material was an old cotton cadet belt. It was also stated that if he had fought back with "a vigorous kick or two" he could have escaped his captors.[7] The reasoning behind Whittaker staging the attack, according to West Point officers, was to gain sympathy in order to prevent him from taking the philosophy examination scheduled in June. Lieutenant Lazelle presented his findings to the superintendent, General Schofield. On April 8, 1880, General Schofield informed Cadet Whittaker of his findings, based on the reports and testimony. Whittaker was stunned by the decision. As he expressed in his letters, he had been confident that the attackers would be caught and brought to justice. He denied having anything to do with the attack and asked for a court of inquiry. A court of inquiry is a group of military officials who investigate a crime committed against military personnel. General Schofield approved Whittaker's request. Schofield published Special Order Number 55 "to examine into and investigate the facts and circumstances connected with the assault upon Cadet Whittaker and the [doubt] cast upon his character in relation thereto."[8] On April 9, 1880, the first session of the court of inquiry began.

General J. M. Schofield (shown here) was the one who informed Cadet Whittaker that officials at West Point felt he had staged the entire attack and inflicted the injuries on himself.

chapter five

THE COURT OF INQUIRY

MILITARY COURT—A court of inquiry consists of three or more military officers who investigate the case and serve as lawyers, and recorders who write down everything that is said in court. All of these officers take an oath to faithfully perform their duties. A court of inquiry makes findings of fact but does not express opinions or make any personal recommendations. The court of inquiry keeps records of its findings and those records are signed by the counsel for the court before being sent to the president of the United States.[1] The biggest difference between a court of inquiry and federal court is that only military personnel can be tried in a court of inquiry. Civilians, people who are not in the military, are tried in federal courts for federal crimes committed against the United States government.

The court of inquiry was held in the Military Academy Library on the grounds of West Point. From the first day, the library was filled with spectators, including newspaper reporters, cadets, and even officers' wives. The library was also filled with buzzing voices as everyone waited for the inquiry to begin.[2]

Cadet Whittaker was the first to testify. The injuries that he had suffered during the attack were still visible. As he walked to the stand, he limped slightly as a result of his injuries. He saluted the officers of the court and was sworn in by Lieutenant Clinton B. Sears, the recorder of the court. Lieutenant Sears asked him to describe the attack. In a strong and steady voice, Whittaker detailed the events of that night. He told the court about the injuries to his face, hands, and feet. The court recorder listened intently to Cadet

Whittaker asked for a court of inquiry following the results of the investigation into the attack. This illustration shows what that court of inquiry looked like.

Whittaker before asking him specific questions about the attack and his life at West Point.

Q: About how high is your bed from the floor?

A: A foot and a half, probably more.

Q: Did the man who jumped upon you place his whole weight on your body, or did he merely throw himself on you and let his feet take the main portion of his weight?

A: It appeared that he sprung into the bed on me, from the feeling at the time that he was actually in the bed.

Q: Where did he place his hands on you?

A: His hands were placed upon my arms.

Q: Indicate to the court where your head was.

A: My head was on my pillow when I was awakened; whether I was lying on my right side or back, I don't remember; but my head was at this part of the alcove and this part of the bed. [Pointing to the diagram]

Q: After seizing your arms what was the next thing this man did?

A: After he had sprung upon me, I was struck on the nose, as I have already stated.

Q: Can you judge the difference between the effect or feeling of the blow of the fist and the effect or feeling produced by some heavy article, as a stick or a bar?

A: I think I can sir.

Q: With what do you think you were struck?

A: In the face with a fist.

Q: You feel sure of that?

A: That is what I think sir. I would imagine that I was not struck with an instrument, but only with a fist.[3]

In Whittaker's room on the morning of the attack there was an Indian club, a wooden club shaped like a large bottle or bowling pin that can be used as a weapon. The court was trying to establish why, if the attackers had carried the club into Whittaker's room, they did not hit him with it. The court was also trying to find a way in which Whittaker himself might have staged the attack. The questioning continued to focus on his injuries and how they were inflicted. On exhibit in the courtroom was a diagram of Whittaker's room, a list of articles found in his room at the time of the attack, and a picture of the position in which Whittaker was found.

The questioning moved to the lighting in the room and the attackers.

Q: Had you at this time noticed the light?

A: I had not, sir.

Q: How long after this did you notice the man with a light?

A: A few minutes after I was struck, I noticed the light and after the man had spoken out.

Q: Where was the man who held the light standing?

A: He remained continually at the foot of the bed as long as he was in the room.

Q: Were you at any time struck with sufficient severity to render you insensible?

A: I don't remember being rendered insensible; I was not rendered insensible by the blows they struck, and the only blows I remember having received were the two blows received in the bed and one with the [mirror].

With this question the court was trying to get Cadet Whittaker to admit that his head injury was not severe. But

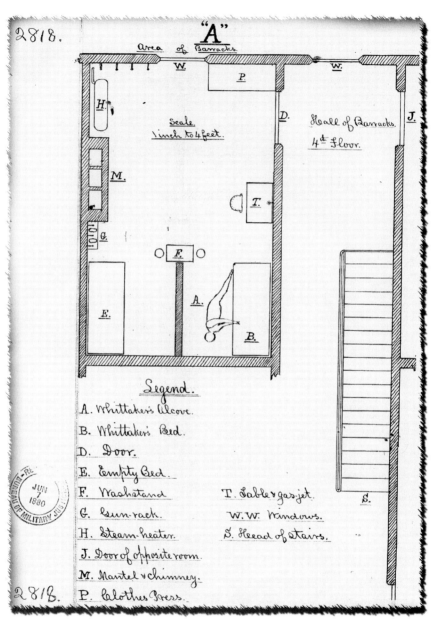

*On exhibit in the courtroom was a diagram of Whittaker's room showing
the position in which Whittaker was found.*

he had suffered a concussion. Of course he would not remember being unconscious. He was, however, unconscious when he was found.

> **Q:** Where was the second blow upon your body struck and with what?
>
> **A:** On the left side of my forehead, on the upper part of my head, but with what it was I don't know. It might have been a fist or some instrument.
>
> **Q:** What do you mean by an instrument? Such as what?
>
> **A:** Such as perhaps a heavy stick or anything of that kind; not an instrument that would probably cut.
>
> **Q:** How were you awakened or brought to consciousness in the morning?
>
> **A:** I was brought to consciousness by the surgeon.[4]

This series of questions continued. Whittaker explained that he did not recognize the voices of the attackers. He did not know for sure whether the attackers were cadets because they had been dressed in civilian clothes.

The questions turned to Whittaker's academic and social life at West Point. During this phase of questioning Whittaker revealed the note of warning he had received a day before the attack—and the fact that it was not the first warning note that he had received.

> **Q:** Had you at any time previous to this ever received any letters similar to this?
>
> **A:** Last fall I received a note similar to this, that is a small envelope and piece of paper and the paper had written upon it the words "look out" without any signature at all or any date or anything else.

Q: What was done with [the note]?

A: I tore it up, sir. I did not think anything of it. I simply destroyed it.

Q: Since you have been a cadet have you ever had any special personal ill treatment. I mean to the extent of physical contact or touch?

A: I have only had two since I have been here.

Cadet Whittaker was referring to the incident with Cadet McDonald, the cadet who hit Whittaker for looking at him, and the attack under investigation.

Q: Have you had any particular trouble or difficulty with any other cadet recently?

A: Not recently, I have not.[5]

As the testimony continued, the court asked questions to try to find a motive for the attack. Cadet Whittaker was a section marker in his philosophy class. He was in charge of making sure the class stayed orderly. The court thought that Whittaker's control over the class might have led to resentment from some of the other cadets.

Q: At any time while you have had your section under your command have you had occasion to speak to any cadet in any way other than the general manner used by section markers?

A: Only in the usual manner; "to pay attention" or "cease talking" or something of that kind but not to say one personally.

Q: Do you remember or know of any occurrence or circumstances that could possibly give rise to any particular feelings of ill will by any cadet?

A: I don't remember. I never reported anyone except one or two cadets, some of them spoke to me about the matter—I should fall into ranks; and last term one of them spoke to me about falling in the company and wanted me to take a different position, and I would not do so.[6]

Whittaker identified Cadet Sergeant Andrus as someone with whom he had had words. During formation, Cadet Andrus did not want Cadet Whittaker to stand next to him.

Q: What words passed between you and him at this time?

A: He told me once or twice not to fall in beside him. The actual words that passed between us, he said, "I told you not to fall in beside me," and I simply said to him, "You can't give me any orders," and fell in at the proper place in dress formation.

Q: Have you any doubt or suspicion or cause for suspecting any party or parties, cadets or others in particular in reference to this occurrence?

A: I do not suspect whom the parties were.

On April 9, 1880, Whittaker began answering more questions about his credibility and character.

Q: Have you any cause to suppose that there is any prejudice against you in the minds of your instructors due to which it would be more difficult for you to graduate than for other cadets against whom such prejudice did not exist?

A: No cause to think so from their actions toward me in the least.

Q: Then you think you have a fair chance to get through as far as your instructors are concerned?

A: Yes, sir, as far as they are concerned.

Q: Has your social isolation had any effect upon you in the progression of your studies?

A: It has sir.[7]

Whittaker's character was on trial. The most important questions in the first two days of the court of inquiry dealt with the accusation that Whittaker staged the entire attack.

Lieutenant Sears said to Whittaker, "You are aware that the opinion held by some is that this assault is entirely an imaginary one and that you alone were involved. Now, for your own benefit I have here this Bible which you state you are accustomed to reading, which has been in your possession for some years, in whose sacredness I presume you have every belief, and I want you to put your hand upon that Bible and take an oath that you do not have any knowledge of and were not involved in the attack." Whittaker placed his hand on his Bible and said, "I do sir [take that oath]."[8]

With this dramatic questioning, Whittaker's passionate testimony, and the circumstantial evidence presented to the court, what conclusion could the court reach? Whittaker had to be found innocent. In the days to come, the questioning and evidence took a different turn, however.

Major Thomas F. Bar from the Judge Advocate General's office in Washington, D.C., arrived at West Point on April 9, 1880. His job was to help evaluate the evidence against Whittaker. He examined Dr. Alexander's report and the note of warning that Whittaker had received. He claimed to notice similarities between Whittaker's handwriting and the handwriting used on the warning note. Based on his opinion, West Point contacted handwriting experts to compare the note of warning with Whittaker's writing. James Gaylor, the superintendent of delivery for the New York Post Office, was one of the experts.[9] He arrived at West Point on April 12, 1880. John G. D. Knight of the Corps of Engineers was appointed at the request of Cadet Whittaker as counsel to assist and advise.

The other handwriting experts included A. S. Southworth of Boston, the oldest and most experienced handwriting expert in the Boston area; John E. Paine, considered the most experienced and well-known expert in New York; and J. E. Hogan of Troy, New York. Hogan was known for using a microscope to examine handwriting. His theory

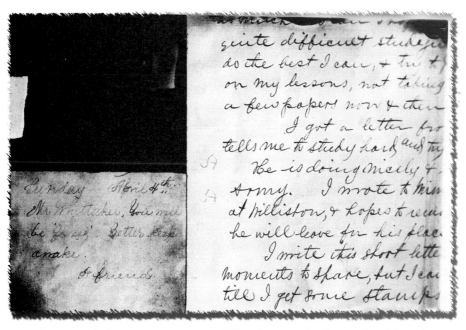

A copy of the anonymous note Whittaker received warning him of trouble (left) and a portion of the letter Whittaker wrote to his mother (right) are shown here.

was that everyone has a specific nerve tremor, which will appear in all handwriting completed by the same person. This tremor is uncontrollable by the writer. The evidence of the tremor can only be seen through a microscope. According to Hogan, this was the most conclusive way to identify different types of handwriting.[10]

To find out who wrote the note, the court asked each cadet in the corps for samples of his handwriting. Approximately three hundred samples were submitted to the court. The court randomly selected samples and numbered them. Whittaker's handwriting sample consisted of letters he had written to his mother and acquaintances, and a note he wrote requesting stamps. Whittaker's samples were labeled number eight. All samples were mixed together and the handwriting on them was compared to the writing on the note of warning.

On the stand, Whittaker was questioned about his hand-writing style. Cadets would generally write their names on their handkerchiefs to identify them and to distinguish them from other handkerchiefs. Whittaker was asked to describe the method he used to mark his handkerchief. This information was important because one of the attackers had placed his handkerchief under Whittaker's ear to stop the blood from flowing. The mark, or initials, used to identify the handkerchief was cut out of the handkerchief found in his room.

Q: What is usually your custom of marking your handkerchief?

A: They're not particularly custom; just as I get the handkerchiefs they are folded. I generally mark them as they are in a good position to write on.

Q: Do you mark them in large letters or in small, coarsely, finely written?

A: I don't know whether you would call it coarse or not. I hardly write a very fine name . . . you can see as I have one here.

Q: Take that [the recorder hands Whittaker a piece of paper and pencil] and write with a pencil the method in which you usually mark your handkerchiefs—about the average size of letters.

A: [Whittaker writes as directed] Something like that, sir.[11]

All cadets were also questioned about the evidence in the case. Each cadet was asked: Have you ever carried any message to or from his [Whittaker's] room? Each cadet answered, "No sir."

While the court of inquiry was in progress, the public became interested in the case. The general feeling was that West Point was focusing too much attention on Cadet Whittaker and not enough on the white cadets. A reporter for *The New York Times* followed the trial, looking for suspects in the attack. One story circulating in the area was that three cadets were overheard plotting the attack the night it occurred. The cadets allegedly said that they were going to "take care of him." This conversation supposedly took place at Ryan's Tavern, a bar in Highland Falls, New York, that many cadets would visit. The owner, Philip Ryan, was called to testify before the court. He denied that the cadets had ever been at the bar. However, a number of cadets testified that they would go there and many times they would change into civilian clothes before going out on the town. On the night of the attack, several cadets were out after curfew. Because of the testimony from cadets, Ryan's testimony was discredited. Instead of investigating this issue further, General Schofield commended the corps of cadets for enduring more questioning—questioning that he thought cast a negative shadow on the cadets.

On April 21, 1880, General Schofield issued an order

West Point cadets in the class of 1874 are shown here. During Cadet Whittaker's trial, the general public felt that too much attention was being focused on Whittaker rather than on the white cadets.

that commended the white cadets "for bearing under the injurious suspicion cast upon them and expressing . . . confidence in their honor and integrity."[12] General Schofield showed by issuing this order before the conclusion of the court of inquiry that he had already made up his mind. He believed that Whittaker had made up the story of being attacked. But what about Whittaker's honor as a member of the corps of cadets? Why was he automatically considered less honorable than the other cadets? Even in the face of serious doubt, General Schofield thought the white cadets were more honorable than Whittaker.

On May 15, 1880, Whittaker was again questioned intensely. Lieutenant Sears asked Whittaker whether he had written the warning note. Whittaker denied writing the note. Sears revealed that one of the handwriting experts had concluded that the warning note and a note Whittaker had written to his mother came from the same sheet of paper. The handwriting expert came to this conclusion because, when placed together, the edges of the pages seemed to match. The expert was alleging that Whittaker tore a sheet of paper in half. On one half, he wrote the warning note; on the other half, he wrote a letter to his mother. It would be revealed later that this expert changed his mind and found that Whittaker had not written the warning note. It appeared, at the time, however, that he was trying to find some way— any way—to convict Whittaker. Whittaker could not provide an explanation for the handwriting expert's conclusion.

Another handwriting expert provided this interpretation of the handwriting samples:

The capital A as used in "April" and as the article proceeding the word "friend." The formation of the "legs" of these letters is similar to that of the A used in the date of the requisition for supplies and in "explanation." The flourishes with which the letters begin have a labored appearance, as though carefully made for the purpose of disguise. I found no A's of this construction in any of the other writings examined.[13]

Based largely on the testimony of three of the five handwriting experts, the court of inquiry reached the following conclusions:

1. The court is unable to believe that such slight wounds as Cadet Whittaker received could have been inflicted by the persons in the manner and under the circumstances described by him.

2. The court does not see why a man with his surroundings, and in his condition and frame of mind, as shown by his own evidence, should have submitted to an assault, such as is alleged, without summoning assistance during the assault or immediately thereafter.

3. The court believes that a person tied as he was, and left as he claims to have been, could readily have released himself had he exerted himself to do so.

4. From the testimony of the post surgeon and others, the court is compelled to believe that Cadet Whittaker was neither asleep nor insensible when he was examined on the morning of April 6, 1880, but that he was [faking it].

B.   B.

from Prof. G. some days ago. It was very encouraging, and I was much pleased to hear from him.

I have been feeling unwell heretofore but I did not go to the hospital, but simply remained away from a few meals, & endeavored to rest the system, & I am all right again.

I found a queer anonymous note in my room yesterday, & 'twas marked from a friend; I don't know what to think of it, & I shall show it to the commandant to-morrow, as it seems a warning against some injury or a threat. 'Tis now nearly nine o'clock & I must soon prepare to retire, as I wish to get up early. We are allowed to get up at 5 o'clock if we desire to study from 5 to 6. I usually go to bed exactly at tatoo & am often up before five o'clock. Since I have received the note I have a queer foreboding of some ill or trick; though I hardly can imagine that the cadets would do me any bodily harm.

Pray that I may do right in all

One of the handwriting experts hired to testify against Cadet Whittaker concluded that the warning note and a note Whittaker had written to his mother came from the same sheet of paper. A portion of Whittaker's letter to his mother is shown here.

5. The court is not able to discover a motive that any person, other than Cadet Whittaker, could have had in making such an assault, and there is no evidence whatsoever to warrant the belief that any other person did make it.

6. The court believes that the hair clippings, the flesh cutting, and the binding could all have been accomplished by Cadet Whittaker himself.

7. The theory that the note of warning is an imitation of Cadet Whittaker's writing is, in the opinion of the court, untenable. The severe tests to which the experts in handwriting were subjected, and their positive testimony, place it beyond doubt that Cadet Whittaker himself wrote the "note of warning," and, therefore, that he is not ignorant of the person or persons engaged in the affair; this latter conclusion is strengthened by the fact that one half of the sheet of paper on which this note is written was found in Cadet Whittaker's possession.

Based on these conclusions, the court wrote the following opinion.

> From the strong array of circumstantial evidence, from the testimony of the experts in handwriting, and from the conflicting statements of Cadet Whittaker and the lack of [truth] evinced by him in certain cases during the investigation, as shown by the evidence, the Court is of the opinion that the imputation upon the character of Cadet Whittaker, referred to in the order convening the Court, and contained in the official reports of the Commandant of Cadets, and the Post Surgeon, is fully sustained.[14]

As incredible as it sounds, the court had found that Cadet Whittaker had inflicted the wounds upon himself. The conclusions were signed by A. Mordecai, Major of Ordnance; Chase W. Raymond, Captain of Engineers; and S. E. Tillman, 1st Lieutenant Corps of Engineers. The report was sent to the Adjutant General of the Army for action against Cadet Whittaker.

Whittaker was surprised and disappointed. However, he did not have time to think about the court's decision. In a few days, June examinations would begin. Despite the ordeal and the pressure he was under, Whittaker passed all of his subjects except philosophy. This is the course that had given him so much trouble and the reason the court gave for his staging the attack.

General Schofield wanted Whittaker to leave West Point to lessen the controversy and media attention. He noted in his private papers, "The only necessity is to get him away from West Point, where he does not belong."[15] Whittaker was expelled based on his failure in philosophy, which led to an indefinite leave of absence from the academy.

Whittaker did not want his character or military career to continue to be damaged. So he took the last step possible in clearing his name. He wrote a letter to the president of the United States, Rutherford B. Hayes, asking for a court-martial. The president had the authority to make the decision for the military academy.

Whittaker wrote: "To his Excellency Rutherford B. Hayes, President of the United States,"

Sir:

Eight long months have passed since a cruel outrage was perpetrated upon me at our National Academy. The facts in my case have, long ago, been made known and the partisan findings of a prejudiced court of inquiry have long ago been given to a public, few of whom can ever believe the bad and malicious accusations made against me. . . .

I have waited particularly till all the excitement has passed—I wait still, it would almost seem, in vain.

I have pleaded, through friends, for a court-martial, hoping that it would give me that justice which a prejudicial court of inquiry has refused.

Friends have asked that I be allowed to resume my studies at the academy, and some have mentioned an appointment in the Army. . . .

To all it seems that a deaf ear has been turned and to this time have I been kept in painful suspense, losing time from my studies.

Now, I ask, what after a harassing cruel trial of nearly eight weeks, bordering on examination, would have done better? What one would have tried harder, in long hours of loneliness like mine, to appear, at examination before an accusing board, and a curious crowd, with nerves unshaken?

Judge me by the testimony of those whom know me from infancy and boyhood; judge me by all my acts at school . . . judge

Cadet Whittaker took every step possible to clear his name. He even wrote a letter to President Rutherford B. Hayes (shown here), to ask for a court-martial.

me by my bearing and character during four years of hatred and worry; judge me by my actions during a very unjust trial, and amid false and malicious accusations. Then turn to the proceedings of the court; see upon what flimsy circumstantial evidence, absurd theories, and nonsensical hypotheses, and mere opinion the findings are based, and ask has even the shadow of justice yet shown me?

Now I ask can I be allowed to resume my studies so as to graduate with the present first class?

Can I receive an appointment in some branch of the military service?

Humbly praying an immediate consideration of the case by your Excellency, I am your humble servant.

Johnson C. Whittaker, U.S. Corps Cadets[16]

Whittaker's honesty and passion prompted President Hayes to issue an order calling for a court-martial.

chapter six

LACK OF TRUST

WEST POINT—Trust, honor, and character are some of the qualities that West Point officers are trained to have. But the main parties involved in the case felt that these qualities were missing in Cadet Whittaker.

In addition to writing letters to his family and friends to vent his emotions, Cadet Whittaker also kept a journal where he could record his true feelings. He described his status in his classes, and why he felt he was receiving such treatment. The following passages were written beginning in September 1878.

First recitation in chemistry was told that my recitation was nonsense. He [referring to the professor] does not seem to like Negros.

In drawing was told by professor that my drawing was ridiculous and he would not correct it. A Negro hater, from what I had before seen of him.

I did pretty well in math but in chemistry was told again my recitation was all nonsense. The instructor does truly hate me. . . .

I shall watch every act and turn of my instructor in chemistry. He has marked me [extremely] low for the last week—a mark too low for my merit and I plainly see now how he hates a Negro. Poor devil, I shall pray for him and all like him.

Did pretty well in chemistry but the instructor did not listen to half of my subject. Consequence: a low mark.

I did pretty well in Philosophy but Lt. S. was harsh on me on account of a little error. He seems like a good man and I think he will treat me fairly.

Today in drawing L. Reed would not correct or approve my drawing; he sent me back to my seat from his desk and said he would come to see it but did not do so. In all the departments I find this term a marked prejudice towards me. . . .

Professor M. in Philosophy scolded me for a slight mistake and was unusually harsh upon me. I am sure I studied the lesson, and if I cannot suit them let me fail. One day will prove all these things.

In chemistry, Lt. J. was savage on me. At every recitation he shows by acts and words that he hates me, but why I cannot say unless it is because I am a Negro.

Did poorly in Philosophy because the instructor gave me a subject or rather a problem in no way connected with the test.[1]

A journal is a place to write private thoughts. It is not meant to be read by other people. However, Whittaker's journal was read in the court of inquiry. Based largely on the things he had written in his journal, the officers thought that Whittaker lacked honor and character; therefore, they did not trust him. His philosophy instructor responded to his journal by saying that Whittaker was treated the same as the other cadets. The subject that he gave Whittaker that Whittaker said was not connected with the test dealt with the study of protons and neutrons. The instructor considered this question "an extra." He said that it was not unusual to give a cadet who shows the ability to apply what he has learned an extra question. He did admit, however, that although he felt the question was connected to the subject, the textbook did not cover the subject.[2] Therefore, Whittaker could not have studied the subject.

The media attention continued during the time between the court of inquiry and the court-martial. For those outside the academy, finding Whittaker guilty was unjust, particularly since his guilt was based on circumstantial evidence, evidence that is not based on facts but rather seems to point to a conclusion. Many newspaper articles mentioned the fact that the academy was putting too much weight on circumstantial evidence. In one article entitled "Circumstantial Evidence," published in the *Stoddart's Review* in August 1880, reporter Benson J. Lossing commented on how flimsy circumstantial evidence was. He explained how other factors, such as prejudices, can influence the delivery of circumstantial evidence which makes it "unsafe as a guide for the judgment in forming an opinion."[3] A court of inquiry is supposed to make sure that it judges only the facts, not opinions.

The conflict between General Schofield and Whittaker really began a month after Whittaker's arrival at West Point. General Schofield thought Whittaker was a coward because he did not fight back when Cadet McDonald hit Whittaker for looking at him. He seemed to use this opinion as a reason to question Whittaker's character. After the court of inquiry, he repeated this opinion: "If you think the rule is taught at West Point that a cadet is to tamely submit to a blow without returning it or defending himself you are greatly mistaken. . . . "[4] General Schofield was criticizing Whittaker for following the rules and being honorable, things that cadets were expected to be also.

General Schofield was a controversial figure, and was removed from his duties as superintendent of West Point on January 21, 1880. General Oliver O. Howard was given the position of superintendent. General Howard held deep religious convictions and a long-standing opposition to slavery. He had been chief of the Freedman's Bureau from 1865 to 1875.[5] The Freedman's Bureau was an agency set up to help African Americans find jobs and homes after slavery. The bureau was also responsible for setting up schools and hospitals for African Americans.

Howard University, the predominately African-American university in Washington, D.C., is named after Oliver O. Howard. Although Howard was white, West Point hoped that his background of helping African Americans and his religious convictions would make African-American cadets at West Point feel more comfortable.

General Oliver O. Howard (shown here) replaced General Schofield as superintendent of West Point on January 21, 1880.

chapter seven

THE COURT-MARTIAL

MILITARY COURT—A court-martial is a court of one or more military officers that judges whether a person subject to military rules has violated military criminal law. If the party on trial is found guilty, it is the court's job to decide what the punishment will be.[1]

The court-martial of Cadet Johnson Whittaker began on February 3, 1881, and took place outside of West Point at the Army Building in New York City. Everyone involved knew that all aspects of the trial would be examined closely.

Therefore, steps were taken to ensure that each step was unbiased. The judge advocate was former West Point professor Major Asa Bird Gardiner. He was the most famous lawyer of that time. Daniel H. Chamberlain, former governor of South Carolina, represented Cadet Whittaker. Whittaker's friend professor Richard Greener also served as Whittaker's support and counsel.

Whittaker faced two charges:

Charge I: "Conduct unbecoming an officer and a

gentleman." The specifics of the charge were that in order to gain public sympathy, to discredit the Military Academy, to escape being suspended from the academy because he was failing philosophy, he cut his ear, hand, and foot with a sharp instrument, tied his feet to his bed rail, tied his hands together, and pretended to have been assaulted and wounded by unknown attackers.

Charge II: "False swearing to the prejudice of good order and military discipline." The specifics of the charge were that he lied under oath about the assault.[2]

The evidence presented at the court-martial was similar to that at the court of inquiry. The focus once again was on the testimony of the handwriting experts. But before the experts testified, General Schofield took the stand to explain why he thought Whittaker was guilty. At first, Schofield had thought Whittaker was innocent. In his journal Schofield stated his outrage and vowed to bring the attackers to justice.[3] His opinion changed when Whittaker asked for a court of inquiry. But, of course, a man accused of staging an attack would want to clear his name. Schofield suggested that Whittaker had outside forces persuading him. Said Schofield, "I did not think that a boy would naturally have so much self-confidence as he displayed. If he had been an old officer, I should not have been surprised at it."[4] Instead of referring to him by his name or by cadet, Schofield used the racially charged word "boy" to describe Whittaker, a man. Once again, General Schofield came to the defense of the white cadets by saying they had been unnecessarily questioned. Schofield's testimony demonstrated what an outcast Whittaker was. It was him against everyone else. The white cadets defended their treatment of Whittaker by saying that he was not shunned because he was black but because the other cadets had the right to choose their friends—and they chose not to befriend him.

Whittaker's defense attorney addressed elements of each of the charges, broke them down, and made a relationship between his treatment, the testimony, and the cross-examination of witnesses. When someone is cross-examined, the lawyer from the opposing side questions a witness about his or her testimony. Chamberlain emphasized how the testimony of more than three hundred people, including cadets, was assumed to be true, without a second thought; however, the testimony of the victim was not and, according to the other side, could not be true.

Next, he showed that Dr. Alexander and another surgeon, Dr. Lippincott, both agreed that Whittaker's wounds had been self-inflicted. They disagreed, however, about where the wounds appeared. If they both saw this differently, perhaps one or both of them could be mistaken about how the wounds had been inflicted and by whom. Chamberlain also focused on the fact that Dr. Alexander thought Whittaker was faking, despite the fact that he had neglected to give Whittaker a complete physical examination after the attack. Then Chamberlain ridiculed the notion that Whittaker could have tied himself up as tightly as he was tied when he was found. He also attacked the opinion of the prosecution that Whittaker had mutilated himself.

Compared to the court of inquiry, the discussion from

the handwriting experts was minimal. However, some strange information did emerge, and once again, the use of a microscope played an important role. A. S. Southworth, the most experienced handwriting expert in Boston, Massachusetts, during that time, claimed to have new evidence to prove that Whittaker had written the warning note. During the court of inquiry, Southworth believed the warning note and a letter Whittaker had written to his mother came from the same sheet of paper. During the court-martial, Southworth claimed to notice "underwriting" on the warning note.

He explained that Whittaker must have folded a piece of paper. On one side he wrote a letter to his mother. When he pressed down on his pencil the imprint of the words were transposed onto the other side of the paper. On this side of the paper, he wrote the warning note before tearing the page in half. Southworth said that when he viewed the warning note under a microscope, he could read words from the letter Whittaker had written to his mother.

Chamberlain had a response for this strange theory. In addition to bringing

Daniel H. Chamberlain, former governor of South Carolina, represented Cadet Whittaker at the court-martial.

in handwriting experts on Whittaker's behalf, he also brought in experts in the correct use of a microscope. They testified that they did not see any "underwriting." Under cross-examination, Southworth and other handwriting experts for West Point did not agree on the words and letters that they alleged were visible. This testimony seemed to damage Southworth's theory.

During the court-martial, Whittaker's letters to family and friends were analyzed. Chamberlain felt it was illegal for the court to use them for this purpose, but the court did not agree. Chamberlain believed that the letters did not have anything to do with the charges brought against Whittaker.

Richard Greener could not address the court during the court-martial because he was not a member of the military. But he did show his support of Whittaker in other ways. In addition to being his friend and providing moral support, he wrote letters to government officials protesting the treatment Whittaker received during the court-martial. Greener complained that, on several occasions during the trial, not all the members of the court were present. He felt this was unfair to Whittaker because not everyone heard all the evidence. Behind the scenes, Greener and Chamberlain disagreed on how Whittaker should be defended. Greener felt that Chamberlain should have done more to target the white cadets, especially during cross-examination.

After several months of testimony, it was time for closing remarks. Chamberlain's summation consisted of 300 pages, emphasizing the government's inability to prove that Whittaker had actually written the warning note. Those in the courtroom were impressed. The spectators in the courtroom applauded as Chamberlain ended.[5]

Now it was the prosecution's turn, but Gardiner did not want to immediately follow Chamberlain's impressive presentation. It would be a hard act to follow, so he asked the court to wait until the following Monday. He cited problems he was experiencing with his voice and a burn he had suffered on his hand that prevented him from taking notes during Chamberlain's summation. On Monday, June 6, 1881, Gardiner presented his summation. He complimented Chamberlain on his presentation and commented, "It is not that there shall be no possibility of a doubt, but that there shall be no *reasonable doubt*."[6] His summation focused on recounting what had happened from the morning Whittaker was discovered—including Dr. Alexander's examination—up to the court of inquiry. He concluded that only Whittaker had a motive for the attack. This motive, he said, had to do with Whittaker being an outcast. What Gardiner did not realize, or would not accept, was that Whittaker was attacked because the white cadets made him an outcast simply because he was black. Nonetheless, Gardiner put the blame for the entire situation on Whittaker.

> He undoubtedly was left alone by many cadets; but whether this occurred because he made himself unpopular by his self-conceit and assumptions or because of certain disagreeable personal peculiarities or because of that want of frankness in his character and appearance which has been manifested here on this witness stand, or whether it was on account of his colored skin merely, or all combined, is something difficult to determine. . . .[7]

Gardiner took this a step further by echoing stereotypical beliefs about African Americans. Gardiner stated, "Negroes are noted for their ability to sham and feign. . . . 'Playing possum' is an Africanism that has come to be generally adopted, and the colored person is, according to all anthropologists endowed with cunning and power of mimicry."[8]

Gardiner closed his summation by repeating the opinion of the handwriting experts. But he also wanted the court to remember other evidence, including the fact that no one admitted to hearing the attack, and the fact that Whittaker's injuries were not considered serious. Gardiner concluded his summation by saying that this evidence showed Whittaker's guilt. Now it was time for the court to deliberate before reaching a verdict.

The academic board of West Point is shown in the library around 1886.

On June 10, 1881, the court announced its decision. Cadet Johnson Chestnut Whittaker was again found guilty on all charges. However, this unusual case did not end there. There were now exceptions to the original charges. The following was deleted from the charges: the accusation that Whittaker had mutilated himself to gain public sympathy; that he wanted to discredit the academy; and that he made up the attack so that he would not have to complete an exam.[9] With these changes gone, how could Whittaker be guilty? The deleted charges were the basis of the prosecution's case. Actually, with these deletions, West Point officials were admitting that there was no basis for the charges. There was no valid reason for Whittaker to have been accused of staging the attack in the first place. But instead of admitting they were wrong and readmitting Whittaker at West Point, the court recommended the following punishment for Whittaker:

> To be dishonorably dismissed from the military services of the United States, and to pay a fine of one dollar, and to be thereafter confined at hard labor for one year in such penitentiary as the reviewing authority may direct.[10]

With this verdict, West Point's position at this time was very clear: under no circumstances was another African-American cadet going to graduate.

A transcript of the court-martial was sent to Judge Advocate General D. E. Swain for his review. In a 101-page report, he cited illegal dealings during the court-martial. For example, he stated that the president of the United States did not have the authority to call for a court-martial. Further, the use of Whittaker's letters as examples of his handwriting, not as evidence, was illegal. He concluded that the prosecution had not proven that Whittaker was the one who had written the warning note or that his wounds had been self-inflicted. The evidence had to be based on facts, not opinions. Swain stated, "On the whole my conclusion is that the prosecution has fallen short of sustaining the charges and specifications by adequate legal proof. . . . [T]he proceedings, findings, and sentence should be, therefore, disapproved."[11]

The secretary of war and the attorney general consulted each other about whether or not Whittaker's letters could be used in the court-martial. Through their consulting and reading military law, they found out the letters should not have been admitted. Therefore, the case against Whittaker was invalid.

On March 22, 1882, President Chester A. Arthur signed an order disapproving the sentence due to improper admission of evidence. Despite the president's disapproval of the proceedings and sentence of the court, Whittaker did not remain at West Point. Secretary of War Robert T. Lincoln ordered Whittaker's dismissal based on his June 1880 grade in philosophy. When Lincoln signed the dismissal papers, Whittaker's life at West Point seemed to have come full circle. Robert T. Lincoln was the son of President Abraham Lincoln. President Lincoln had signed the Emancipation Proclamation, which had helped make it possible for Whittaker to attend West Point. Lincoln's son signed the dismissal papers that made it impossible for Whittaker to

President Chester A. Arthur signed an order on March 22, 1882, disapproving the sentence against Cadet Whittaker, due to improper admission of evidence.

graduate from West Point. Whittaker never received what he had worked so hard and endured so much for: a commission to continue serving in the U.S. military.

Whittaker's character and perseverance did not let this ordeal stop him from succeeding in life. In his only public speech about his life at West Point, Whittaker said, "With God as my guide, duty as my watchword, I can, I must, and I will, win a place in life."[12] And he did just that.

He received a law degree from South Carolina College. He practiced law in Sumter, South Carolina, in 1885. After that, he became a teacher at the Colored Normal, Industrial, Agricultural and Mechanical College of South Carolina, now known as South Carolina State University. He married Page Harrison of Sumter. They had two sons, Miller and John.

Jim Crow Laws

Whittaker wanted his family to escape from the Jim Crow laws of the South; so in 1908, the Whittaker family moved to Oklahoma City, Oklahoma. While there, Johnson Whittaker worked as a teacher, and later, a principal at Frederick Douglass High School.

Jim Crow laws were passed between 1890 and 1910 by Southern states to separate blacks and whites in public places such as restaurants, schools, public transportation, and even at water fountains. The laws were intended to create separate facilities for both races so that whites would not come into direct contact with blacks. Signs that said "Whites Only" and "Colored Only" were posted to further highlight the separation of races. If blacks saw a sign that read "Whites Only," they knew they could not enter. If they did, they would be insulted, and perhaps assaulted, by whites.

Another extremely racist element of these laws was the fact that African Americans could not vote, even though the Fifteenth Amendment to the United States Constitution protected voting rights. State government made provisions in the laws for requirements that they knew would not allow African Americans to vote. The requirements included owning property, such as a house, and being able to read and write. Unfortunately during this time many African Americans were not given the opportunity to acquire property and many could not read or write. Even those who fulfilled the requirements were often prevented from voting by intimidation from white officials.

The Whittaker family was part of a group of thousands of African Americans who migrated to states in the Midwest and the Plains. In this case, migration refers to a group of people who travel together to reach the same location.

Those, like the Whittakers, who migrated west were known as "Exodusters." This word comes from combining Exodus, one of the books of the Bible, with "dusters," which refers to the dust bowl or flatlands of the Midwest.

Despite the fact that African Americans had more opportunities in the Midwest than they did in the South, prejudice still existed. In Oklahoma, the Whittakers faced racism. Shots were fired at their home and a cross was burned in their front yard. This treatment of the family changed when

Cadet Johnson Whittaker did not let his experience at West Point stop him from succeeding in life. He went on to practice law and later became a teacher at the Colored Normal, Industrial, Agricultural and Mechanical College of South Carolina. He is shown here (top row, far right) with other instructors.

a reporter wrote an article about Johnson Whittaker and mentioned that Whittaker and his sons were sharpshooters.[13]

Tulsa, Oklahoma, is approximately one hundred miles from Oklahoma City. An event in Tulsa would lead Whittaker to make a major decision for his family.

As more African Americans moved to Tulsa and became successful, the racial tension between blacks and whites grew. More and more blacks accused of crimes were being kidnapped from jails and lynched before a trial could be conducted.

Nineteen-year-old Dick Rowland, who was black, was accused of attacking Sarah Page, a seventeen-year-old white girl. Conflicting stories emerged about what had happened. The alleged attack occurred in the elevator of the Drexel building were she was an elevator operator and he shined shoes. While the police were investigating the attack, the local newspaper, *Tribune*, published sensational stories about the attack. The focus of the stories was on the races of the alleged attacker and victim. This would sell papers.

During this period in the United States, a black man was not allowed to speak to a white woman, much less be close enough to be accused of assaulting her. Many white men held the racist attitude that a black man was not worthy of coming into contact with a white woman—that doing so would damage her honor. Many times, black men would be arrested or lynched simply for looking at a white woman.

Within forty-five minutes after the paper reached the public, there was talk of lynching Rowland, and large crowds of whites began to gather in downtown Tulsa, outside the courthouse. The crowd was estimated at two thousand. Some seventy-five of the people protesting were black, the rest were white. The police asked both groups to leave. The black men were in the process of leaving when they were confronted by the whites. Shots were fired and the Tulsa Race Riot of 1921 began.[14]

The white mob went to the black section of Tulsa known as Greenwood. More than one thousand homes and businesses were destroyed by fire and theft. African-American churches were also destroyed. Blacks and whites were killed; sixty-five whites were arrested. Approximately six thousand African Americans were displaced or otherwise affected by the riot.[15]

The incident that had sparked the riot ended when Sarah Page refused to prosecute and the charges against Dick Rowland were dropped. But, the race riot in Tulsa caused racial tensions throughout Oklahoma to escalate. Despite the fact that the South still had oppressive Jim Crow laws, the Whittakers felt that their lives would be better in their home state of South Carolina. So, they moved back to South Carolina in 1925. Johnson

This portrait of Johnson Whittaker was probably done in the 1920s.

Whittaker returned to the Colored Normal, Industrial, Agriculture and Mechanical College. This time he taught chemistry, psychology, and military science.

Whittaker instilled in his sons the importance of self-confidence and education. Both sons were commissioned officers in the Army during World War I. Miller Whittaker became the third president of South Carolina State College. John Whittaker became the first African-American engineer in South Carolina, and designed the major transportation routes in Detroit, Michigan. The Whittaker family was expected to do well in life. The family's achievements extended to Whittaker's grandson, Peter. During World War II, Peter Whittaker was a member of the Tuskegee Airmen, the first African-American fighter pilots in the military.

The Tuskegee Airmen unit was formed so that African Americans could train as pilots. During World War II the U.S. Army was segregated. Black pilots could not train together with white pilots. The Tuskegee Airmen completed Army flight classroom instruction and numerous hours of flight time in Tuskegee, Alabama. Approximately one thousand African-American men earned their wings—a pin worn by the pilots to show that they were qualified to fly a plane. Nearly five hundred Tuskegee Airmen flew as combat mission fighter pilots.

Johnson Whittaker's great-grandson Ulysses was a lieutenant in the Army and a Harvard-educated lawyer. He is also a judge of the Third Judicial Circuit Court in Detroit, Michigan. Johnson Whittaker would have been proud. In an interview with *The New York Times* in 1994, Peter

Whittaker's daughter, Cecil Whittaker McFadden, said of her great-grandfather, Johnson Whittaker, "He inspired the rest of us, and we've done very well."[16]

In 1931, Johnson Whittaker died of a bleeding ulcer. His great-granddaughter attributed his illness to his refusal to discuss his treatment at West Point and the details of the court-martial. She stated, "I think holding it all in like that, well, it was hard to go on."[17] Johnson Whittaker never discussed the details of the West Point attack with his family. "He burned all the papers about it because he did not

The Tuskegee Airmen were the first African-American fighter pilots in the military during World War II. Cadet Whittaker's grandson, Peter (not shown), was a member.

want his sons to grow up bitter."[18] McFadden was thirteen years old when her great-grandfather died. She did not even find out that her great-grandfather had attended West Point until she was twenty-three years old, when her mother told her. Johnson Whittaker's life serves as a source of inspiration not only for the Whittaker family but also for all Americans. He had the courage, strength, and character to overcome adversity with dignity.

Johnson Chestnut Whittaker is buried in Orangeburg, South Carolina. His burial ground is a historic site that can be visited by the public.

chapter eight

WHERE WE ARE TODAY

AFTERMATH—As the years passed, steps were taken to integrate the military and society. But prejudice and segregation continued. Three years after the Whittaker court-martial, the Supreme Court declared the Civil Rights Act of 1875 invalid. The act called for the equal treatment of everyone in the United States regardless of a person's place of birth, race, color, religion, or politics. Equal treatment included the use of public places such as hotels, theaters, and restaurants by blacks and whites.[1] According to the Supreme Court's decision, black people could be excluded from white schools, jobs, theaters, and restaurants.

West Point was still trying to change its attitude and the treatment that African-American cadets received. Ten years after Henry O. Flipper graduated, the next African American to graduate was John H. Alexander of Helena, Arkansas, on June 12, 1887.

Charles Young of

Mayslick, Kentucky, was the next African-American cadet to enter West Point, in 1894. During his first year at the academy he failed math, which resulted in his dismissal. But Lieutenant George Goethals, his engineering instructor, asked West Point to reconsider, and West Point officials decided to give Young another chance. Lieutenant Goethals helped Young study so that he would be ready for his examination. Young did well on the reexamination and was readmitted. He continued to do well in all of his classes and graduated from West Point on August 31, 1899. It would be another forty years before the next African-American cadet would enter West Point.

By the start of the twentieth century, eighteen states in the North and West had laws in place to protect African Americans from racial discrimination. However, in the South especially, racial discrimination was still openly practiced.

The National Association for the Advancement of Colored People (NAACP) was founded in 1909. It quickly became the leading organization in the struggle for equal treatment of African Americans. The NAACP challenged discrimination and illegal treatment of African Americans through the legal system. The NAACP's Legal Defense Fund was set up for this purpose. Thurgood Marshall, who became a Justice of the U.S. Supreme Court in 1967, began his law career with the NAACP's Legal Defense Fund.

In 1941, President Franklin D. Roosevelt signed Executive Order 8802 to desegregate government defense contracts. Desegregation ended separation based on race.

African Americans had to be considered for employment with companies that completed work for the government.[2]

The military's nondiscrimination policy was created by President Harry Truman on July 26, 1948. The order states that all people in the armed services should be treated equally without regard to race, color, religion, or nationality. Truman's order was intended to bring about social change and military inclusion of African Americans. Many blacks joined the military thinking that whites would treat them with respect. As society changed and the push for integration grew, African Americans demanded equality in the military. During World War II, African Americans composed one eighth of the enrollment in the U.S. armed forces.[3] President Truman's order improved conditions for African Americans in the military.

Brown v. *Board of Education of Topeka, Kansas*, in 1954 was a groundbreaking civil rights case. It challenged segregation in public education by eliminating local, state, and federal segregation laws in public education. Segregation continued, however, in other areas of public life. Rosa

President Franklin D. Roosevelt signed Executive Order 8802 in 1941 to desegregate government contracts.

Parks's experience on a bus in 1955 proved that segregation was still thriving.

Parks and her husband, Raymond, had been members of the Montgomery, Alabama, branch of the NAACP for many years. In 1943, Rosa Parks became the secretary for the Montgomery branch. In 1943 and 1945 she tried to register to vote. She was turned away by racist voting laws. Her desire to be treated equally and with respect created a defining moment in the civil rights movement in the United States.

On December 1, 1955, Rosa Parks was riding home from work on the public bus line in Montgomery. Montgomery had Jim Crow laws in place, so she was sitting in the first row of the "colored" section of the bus. When a white man got on the bus, he discovered there were no seats left in the "white" section. He told Parks to move to the back of the bus so that he could have her seat closer to the front of the bus. Parks refused to move. Even with the man and the bus driver using rude and abusive language, she did not budge. The bus driver would not continue to drive the bus and he called the police. Simply because Parks refused to sit in the back of the bus, she was arrested and convicted of violating Alabama's segregation laws. She was fined ten dollars and had to pay an additional four dollars in court costs.[4]

Rosa Parks's nonviolent protest against segregation laws led to a boycott by African Americans of the Montgomery public bus system. A boycott occurs when people come together to refuse to buy, sell, or use something. Within a day of Parks's arrest, the Montgomery chapter of the

NAACP had organized the boycott. It had the support of fifty thousand African Americans in Montgomery.[5] They were tired of the unfair treatment they received from the bus line and the rude treatment from the white drivers. During the boycott, African Americans supported each other in finding other means of transportation.

The boycott lasted for more than a year and brought to the attention of people all over the United States the unfair treatment of African Americans in the South. In November 1956, a federal court ordered that Montgomery buses be desegregated. The boycott had been a success. Rosa Parks's courage had made a huge difference in the treatment of African Americans in Montgomery, Alabama. But Parks and other boycotters paid a price for their courage. They were subjected to violence from whites. Parks and her husband lost their jobs and were harassed and threatened. They moved to Detroit, Michigan, to escape this treatment. Rosa Parks continued to be involved with the NAACP in Detroit.

Although Rosa Parks's actions created huge gains in the civil rights movement, there was still a long way to go toward achieving equal rights for all. As a result of the Montgomery boycott, an organization called the Montgomery Improvement Association (MIA) was formed. The leader of that group was a young minister named Dr. Martin Luther King, Jr. He had just moved to Montgomery from Atlanta, Georgia, to become the pastor of Dexter Avenue Baptist Church.

As a student at Boston University, he studied the nonviolent protest methods of Mohandas Gandhi. Gandhi was an Indian leader who believed in changing a legal and political system through nonviolent marches, demonstrations, and boycotts. King believed nonviolent protests would lead to better treatment for African Americans. He brought the African-American community in Montgomery together with his message of nonviolent protest and his magnetic public speaking abilities. Soon his leadership would extend throughout the United States.

King was instrumental in leading many nonviolent protests. In 1957 he founded the Southern Christian Leadership Conference (SCLC). The SCLC consisted of African-American ministers and church members in southern states. King visited churches to preach his message of nonviolence for racial equality. The goal of the SCLC was to challenge racial segregation. This message reached whites in northern states. Many provided financial support and advice to spread the message of the importance of racial equality. The financial support helped to pay bail for protesters who were jailed for demonstrating peacefully.

In 1959 King, his wife, Coretta, and their four children moved back to Atlanta where he became the co-pastor of Ebenezer Baptist Church. His father, Martin Luther King II, was the pastor of the church.

The Height of the Civil Rights Movement

The 1960s were a time of tremendous social change. With the introduction of television into many American homes, people everywhere could see for themselves the struggle for equal rights. Demonstrations organized by the SCLC against hotels, housing, restaurants, and transportation that would not allow blacks were televised nightly. One of the most terrifying events to be televised occurred in 1965 in Birmingham, Alabama. Martin Luther King encouraged children and teenagers to get involved in the civil rights struggle. On this day, hundreds of children marched peacefully through the streets of downtown Birmingham. They sang gospel and civil rights songs as they marched.

Birmingham's police commissioner, Eugene "Bull" Connor, was against desegregation. The sight of the young protesters really angered him. To end the demonstration, he ordered police officers to spray protesters with water from high-pressured fire hoses and to let dogs loose to attack the protesters. Images of children screaming, running, hiding, and kneeling with their arms covering their heads in an effort to protect themselves were broadcast for all Americans to see. These upsetting images resulted in increased support for the civil rights movement. Some of the children were sent to jail. Dr. King believed that even children had the moral right and responsibility to disobey unjust laws. Many Americans

Dr. Martin Luther King, Jr., brought his belief in nonviolent protest methods to the civil rights movement.

agreed with him and they showed their support by campaigning against segregation laws.[6]

That support for civil rights was shown when more than two hundred thousand people attended a march on Washington on August 28, 1963. The march was organized by Martin Luther King and other African-American leaders. At the march, King recited his most famous "I Have a Dream" speech. He eloquently expressed the need for social equality: "I have a dream that my four little children will one day live in a nation where they will not be judged by the color of their skin but by the content of their character."

A variety of nonviolent protests and Martin Luther King's powerful speeches paved the way for the Civil Rights Act of 1964. This act enforced every American's constitutional right to vote, regardless of race, color, religion, gender, or nationality. It also ensured that discrimination would not be accepted in public places. In addition, the act gave the attorney general of the United States the right to sue businesses that did not follow the act's guidelines. Any program that received assistance from the federal government had to follow the guidelines of the act. Martin Luther King was awarded the Nobel Prize for Peace in 1964. Every year the prize is awarded to a person or several people whose actions make the world a safer place for everyone.

But there was more work to be done to ensure that the new Civil Rights Act would be followed. By 1965, Alabama still did not allow African Americans to vote. The SCLC organized a protest march to demonstrate that Alabama had biased voting laws and did not enforce the Civil Rights Act.

The march began in Selma, Alabama. The final destination of the marchers was Montgomery, Alabama, about fifty miles away. Before they could get completely out of Selma, the marchers were met with violence. Once again, television reporters were there to broadcast to the nation this unjust treatment. Martin Luther King organized another march, and two weeks later three thousand marchers were on their way to Montgomery. This time, they were protected by police and the federal government. The Selma marchers and twenty thousand other marchers from various locations arrived in Montgomery where Martin Luther King addressed the crowd. African Americans were finally able to vote in Alabama.

King's nonviolent fight for social equality continued until he was shot and killed on April 4, 1968. His legacy—a nonviolent approach to gaining and improving the social rights of African Americans—will remain forever.

Equal Opportunity and Affirmative Action

The Equal Employment Opportunity Commission (EEOC), a government agency, was established as part of the Civil Rights Act of 1964. It ensures that federal laws prohibiting employment discrimination are followed. Individuals who believe they have been discriminated against in their place of employment can go to the EEOC to file charges against their employer. The EEOC will investigate the charges to determine if discrimination took place. The EEOC will also try to help the person who filed the complaint and the employer to solve the dispute. If they cannot, the EEOC may bring suit in federal court on behalf of the employee alleging discrimination.[7]

President John F. Kennedy was the first person to use the phrase "affirmative action," when he issued Executive Order 10952 in 1961. The order directed federal contractors to "take affirmative action to ensure the applicants are employed, and employees are treated during their employment, without regard to race, creed, color or national origin."[8] Since then, affirmative action has come to refer to policies aimed at increasing the numbers of people from certain minority groups in employment, education, business, government, and other areas of public life. In general, affirmative action is intended to benefit groups that are thought to have suffered from discrimination.

In the last forty years, affirmative action has gone through many changes. Recently, there has been a push to eliminate affirmative action completely. States such as California and Washington have asked voters to reject state affirmative action laws. Some people believe that laws are not needed because opportunities exist for everyone without government intervention. Others believe that affirmative action gives unfair advantages to those minority groups it targets. The topic of affirmative action will surely continue to be debated.

Conditions in the United States in general and at West Point specifically have changed dramatically since Cadet Whittaker's time more than a century ago. West Point now has approximately four thousand men and women cadets. Women were first admitted to West Point in 1976. The majority of appointments are still based on nominations by United States senators and representatives. But now, career military personnel can also nominate cadets. If qualified, citizens from the Philippines, Canada, and some Latin American countries may be admitted to the academy.[9] West Point's officers protect the interests of the United States all over the world. Those officers must reflect the diversity of the United States. Said former Commander of Cadets General Robert St. Onge, Jr., "West Point works hard to get a solid balance of minorities as well as men and women, because it must represent the nation."[10]

West Point's mission has also changed since Whittaker attended. Today, the mission of the Brigade Tactical Department is to "develop, train, and inspire cadets, through integration of the academy programs, to be leaders of character; committed to duty, honor, country, and inspired for careers as United States Army officers and a lifetime of selfless service to the Nation."[11] In order to accomplish this goal, the academy has incorporated a variety of programs. Some programs focus on the cadet as an individual and expand his or her academic, military, physical, and moral-ethical potential.[12] The programs also gives cadets more responsibility for themselves and the cadet corps. "Duty, honor, country." This is the motto all cadets must live by. Their code of conduct is, "A cadet will not lie, steal, cheat or tolerate those who do."[13]

A wrong was finally righted at West Point when, in January 1994, United States Senator Fritz Hollings of South Carolina introduced a bill to grant a posthumous commission to Whittaker. A posthumous commission would recognize Johnson Whittaker's accomplishments even after his death. The honor that Hollings wanted Whittaker to have was that of a Second Lieutenant. "I hope that in some way that making Mr. Whittaker an officer posthumously will right a wrong done to him more than one hundred years ago," said Hollings.[14]

Conditions at West Point have changed dramatically since Cadet Whittaker attended more than a century ago.

The bill made its way through Congress and onto President Bill Clinton's desk. On July 24, 1995, a posthumous commission ceremony for Cadet Johnson Whittaker took place. Senator Hollings and many other politicians were present. President Clinton discussed Whittaker's achievements and the importance of what he had endured and accomplished. Said President Clinton:

> Johnson Whittaker was a rare individual, a pathfinder, a man who, through courage, example, and perseverance, paved the way for future generations of African-American military leaders: General Chappie James, Lt. General Benjamin O. Davis . . . General Colin Powell, and so many others. In part because Whittaker and others like him took those first brave steps, America's Armed Forces today serve as a model for equal opportunity to our entire country, and indeed, the world.
>
> We cannot undo history. But today, finally, we can pay tribute to a great American, and we can acknowledge a great injustice.[15]

President Clinton presented Johnson Whittaker's Bible to his great-granddaughter, Cecil Whittaker MacFarland. The Bible had been kept with the official records of the court-martial. Next, President Clinton presented the Whittaker family with the bars that Johnson Whittaker would have earned as an officer. The bars indicate a soldier's rank in the military and are stitched on a patch that a soldier wears on the sleeve of his uniform. President Clinton further stated, "May God bless his memory, and may all of us honor his service to the United States of America."[16]

Cadet Johnson Chestnut Whittaker and cultural pioneers like him have helped pave the way for African Americans and many other minorities to succeed in life. What he went through set the stage for more accepting and tolerant attitudes. Cadet Johnson Chestnut Whittaker is a true hero and a classic example that even when faced with severe obstacles, people can persevere and achieve their goals.

Attitudes about racial equality have improved over the years. There is much, however, that still needs to be accomplished. One way to combat racism is to realize that no one benefits from it. One of the best ways to overcome racism is to learn to appreciate different cultures, and to realize that everyone is an individual within a culture. Treating others the way we wish to be treated is one giant step along the path to better understanding among all people.

Questions for Discussion

1. Do you think equal opportunity and affirmative action laws should be eliminated? Explain your answer.

2. What can be done to help prevent a situation like Whittaker's from happening again?

3. There is a concept called "group think" that says everyone in a group will agree on a subject simply to avoid conflict. How could "group think" have affected the outcome of the court of inquiry and the court-martial? Explain your answer.

4. What can we do to overcome some of the problems associated with racism?

5. What should Superintendent Schofield and the other officers have done differently to ensure that justice was served and the correct people were punished in the Whittaker case?

6. How are Johnson Whittaker and Martin Luther King, Jr., alike? Explain your answer.

7. After slavery, the United States tried to provide opportunities for African Americans during Reconstruction. What could have been done differently?

Chapter Notes

Chapter 1. The Attack

1. "RG Records of the Office of the Judge Advocate," QQ1858, Part 1, National Archives, April 9–10, 1880, pp. 5–8.

2. Ibid.

3. Ibid.

Chapter 2. Racism in the Making

1. Peter J. Parish, *Slavery: History and Historians* (New York: Harper and Row Publishers, 1989), p. 15.

2. Ibid., p. 17.

3. C. Vann Woodward, ed., *Mary Chestnut's Civil War* (New Haven, Conn.: Yale University Press, 1981), p. 251.

4. Mary Frances Berry, *Military Necessity and Civil Rights Policy* (Port Washington, N.Y.: Kennikat Press, 1977), p. 93.

5. National Archives and Records Administration, "The Fight for Equal Rights: Black Soldiers in the Civil War," February 9, 1999, <http://www.nara.gov/education/teaching/usct/home.html> (September 8, 2000).

Chapter 3. Setting the Stage

1. C. Vann Woodward, ed., *Mary Chestnut's Civil War* (New Haven, Conn.: Yale University Press, 1981), p. 243.

2. E. Merton Coulter, *The South During Reconstruction: 1865–1877* (Baton Rouge, La.: Louisiana State University Press, 1947), p. 319.

3. "United States Military Academy," *Encyclopedia Britannica Online*, © 2000, <http://www.britannica.com> (September 8, 2000).

4. Ibid.

5. Henry Ossian Flipper, *The Colored Cadet at West Point* (New York: Arno Press, 1969), p. 33.

6. Office of Deputy Assistant Secretary of Defense, "Black Americans in Defense of Our Nation: Chapter Six, The United States Military Academy," U.S. History, September 1, 1990 <http://www.elibrary.com/s/edumark/getd...id=1129039@library_a&dtype=0~0&dinst=0> (July 1, 2000).

7. Ibid.

8. Thomas J. Fleming, *West Point: The Men and Times of the United States Military Academy* (New York: William Morrow and Company, 1969), p. 217.

9. Ibid.

10. Ibid., p. 218.

11. Ibid., p. 219.

12. Office of Deputy Assistant Secretary of Defense, "Black Americans in Defense of Our Nation: Chapter Six, The United States Military Academy."

13. Flipper, p. i.

14. Ibid., p. 120.

15. Ibid.

16. Ibid.

17. Charles Pope, "Clinton Tries to Right 115-Year-Old Wrong," *The State*, (Columbia, S.C.) July 25, 1995, p. A1.

18. "RG Records of the Office of the Judge Advocate," QQ1858, Part 1, National Archives, April 9–10, 1880, p. 2657.

19. Ibid.

Chapter 4. The Investigation

1. "RG Records of the Office of the Judge Advocate," QQ1858, Part I, National Archives, April 9–10, 1880, p. 7380.

2. John F. Marszalek, "A Black Cadet At West Point," *American Heritage*, August 1971, p. 32.

3. Ibid.

4. "RG Records of the Office of the Judge Advocate," QQ1858, Part XI, National Archives, April 9–10, 1880, Appendix.

5. Ibid.

6. Ibid.

7. Ibid.

8. Ibid.

Chapter 5. The Court of Inquiry

1. Glossary of Military Terms, Phrases, Abbreviations, Slang <http://hometown.aol.com/usmilbrats/glossary/index.html> (September 8, 2000).

2. John F. Marszalek, "A Black Cadet At West Point," *American Heritage*, August 1971, p. 35.

3. "RG Records of the Office of the Judge Advocate," QQ1858, Part I, National Archives, April 9–10, 1880, p. 13.

4. Ibid.

5. Ibid.

6. Ibid.

7. Ibid.

8. Marszalek, p. 35.

9. "Conclusion of the Whittaker Investigation at West Point," *Penman's Art Journal*, June 1880, p. 44.

10. Ibid.

11. "RG Records of the Office of the Judge Advocate," QQ1858, Part I, National Archives, April 9-10, 1880, p. 43.

12. Library of Congress, John M. Schofield, "Letters Sent USMA, West Point 1877–1881," container number 50.

13. "Conclusion of the Whittaker Investigation at West Point," p. 45.

14. "RG Records of the Office of the Judge Advocate," QQ1858, Part I, National Archives, April 9–10, 1880, p. 2814.

15. Library of Congress, John M. Schofield, "Letters Sent USMA, West Point 1877–1881," container number 50.

16. "RG Records of the Office of the Judge Advocate," QQ1858, Part I, National Archives, April 9–10, 1880, p. 12950.

Chapter 6. Lack of Trust

1. "RG Records of the Office of the Judge Advocate," QQ1858, Part I, National Archives, April 9–10, 1880, p. 2654.

2. Ibid., p. 2658.

3. Benson J. Lossing, "Circumstantial Evidence," *Stoddart's Review*, August 1880, p. 123.

4. John F. Marszalek, "A Black Cadet At West Point," *American Heritage*, August 1971, p. 36.

5. Russell F. Weigley, *History of the United States Army* (New York: The Macmillan Company, 1967), p. 257.

Chapter 7. The Court Martial

1. General Court-Martial Orders, Number 18, Headquarters of the Army, Adjutant General's Office, Washington, March 22, 1882.

2. Library of Congress, John M. Schofield, "Letters Sent USMA, West Point 1877–1881," container number 50.

3. Ibid.

4. Ibid.

5. John F. Marszalek, "A Black Cadet At West Point," *American Heritage*, August 1971, p. 105.

6. Ibid.

7. Ibid.

8. General Court-Martial Orders, Number 18, Headquarters of the Army, Adjutant General's Office, Washington, March 22, 1882.

9. Ibid.

10. Ibid.

11. "Seeking 'Fair Deal' for a Black Cadet," *The New York Times*, January 31, 1994, p. 1.

12. Ibid.

13. Karl F. Davie Burgdorf, "Our People: Johnson C. Whittaker: The Professor Had Been Assaulted," *Carologue*, Autumn 1994, p. 3.

14. Scott Ellsworth, *Death in a Promised Land* (Baton Rouge, La.: Louisiana State University Press, 1982), pp. 45–53.

15. Ibid., pp. 53–70.

16. "Seeking 'Fair Deal' for a Black Cadet," p. 1.

17. Ibid.

18. Ibid.

Chapter 8. Where We Are Today

1. "The Civil Rights Act of March 1, 1875," February 22, 1997, <http://chnm.gmu.edu/courses/122/recon/civilrightsact.html> (September 8, 2000).

2. Americans United for Affirmative Action, "Affirmative Action: A Timeline—1776–1899: Reconstruction to Jim Crow," <http://www.auaa.org/timeline/index.html> (September 8, 2000).

3. Russell F. Weigley, *History of the United States Army* (New York: The Macmillan Company, 1967), p. 555.

4. Microsoft Encarta Online Encyclopedia, "Civil Rights Movement in the United States," © 2000 <http://encarta.msn.com/find/concise.asp?z=1&pg=2&ti=761580647> (September 8, 2000).

5. Ibid.

6. Ibid.

7. "U.S. Equal Employment Opportunity Commission: An Overview," November 3, 1997, <http://www.eeoc.gov/overview.html> (September 8, 2000).

8. "Americans United for Affirmative Action: A Timeline—1776–1899: Reconstruction to Jim Crow."

9. Encyclopedia Britannica Online, "United States Military Academy," © 2000 <http://search.eb.com/bol/topic?eu= 76282&sctn=1&pm=1> (September 8, 2000).

10. Larry Smith "Duty, Honor, Country," *Parade*, May 7, 2000, p. 8.

11. Ibid.

12. Ibid.

13. Ibid., p. 7.

14. Encyclopedia Britannica Online, "United States Military Academy," © 2000.

15. "Remarks at the Posthumous Commissioning Ceremony for Johnson C. Whittaker," Weekly Compilation of Presidential Documents, Washington, D.C., July 13, 1995, President Bill Clinton. <http://proquest.umi.com/pqdweb?TS=9428...&Dtp=1&Did=000000006800490&Mtd=1&Fmt=3> (November 17, 1999).

16. Ibid.

Glossary

abolitionists—People who wanted to end slavery.

affirmative action—Policies aimed at increasing the numbers of people from certain social and racial groups in employment, education, business, government, and other areas of public life.

boycott—People coming together to refuse to buy, sell, or use something.

circumstantial evidence—Evidence that is not based on facts but rather seems to point to a conclusion.

commissioned officers—A group of military officers having the authority to hold rank over an enlisted person.

court-martial—A group of military officers that is appointed by a commander to try military personnel for offenses committed under military law. The officers decide whether military law has been violated.

court of inquiry—A group of military officials who investigate the circumstances of a crime committed against military personnel.

cross-examine—Questioning a trial witness by the opposing counsel.

demerits—Marks recorded against a student for a fault in behavior or appearance.

desegregate (desegregation)—To end separation based on race.

Emancipation Proclamation—An order signed by President Abraham Lincoln that led to the freeing of slaves after the Civil War.

Freedman's Bureau—An agency set up to help African Americans find jobs and homes after slavery. The bureau was also responsible for setting up schools and hospitals for African Americans.

integrate (integration)—To open up to people of all races.

Jim Crow laws—Laws to separate blacks and whites in public locations such as restaurants, schools, public transportation, and even water fountains.

military academy—A school that educates and trains students in military discipline, in an effort to prepare them for military service.

posthumous commission—A military honor recognizing an individual's accomplishments presented after death.

Reconstruction—The period between 1865 and 1877 when Southern states were reorganized to again become part of the Union of the United States.

reveille—A signal given in the morning to awaken soldiers. Usually the signal comes in the form of a soldier blowing a horn or bugle.

stereotype—To unfairly assign a negative, prejudiced judgment to a whole group of people.

Tuskegee Airmen—The first African-American fighter pilots in the United States military.

wings—A pin worn by pilots to show that they are qualified to fly a plane.

Further Reading

Banfield, Susan. *The Fifteenth Amendment: African-American Men's Right to Vote.* Springfield, N.J.: Enslow Publishers, Inc., 1998.

Fireside, Harvey. *Plessy v. Ferguson: Separate But Equal?* Springfield, N.J.: Enslow Publishers, Inc., 1997.

Fireside, Harvey, and Sarah Betsy Fuller. *Brown v. Board of Education: Equal Schooling for All.* Hillside, N.J.: Enslow Publishers, Inc., 1994.

Herda, D.J. *The Dred Scott Case: Slavery and Citizenship.* Hillside, N.J.: Enslow Publishers, Inc., 1994.

Kent, Zachary. *The Civil War: "A House Divided."* Hillside, N.J.: Enslow Publishers, Inc., 1994.

Lucas, Eileen. *Civil Rights: The Long Struggle.* Springfield, N.J.: Enslow Publishers, Inc., 1996.

Marszalek, John F. *Assault at West Point.* New York: Collier, 1994.

Newman, Gerald, and Eleanor Newman Layfield. *Racism: Divided by Color.* Springfield, N.J.: Enslow Publishers, Inc., 1995.

Schleichert, Elizabeth. *The Thirteenth Amendment: Ending Slavery.* Springfield, N.J.: Enslow Publishers, Inc., 1998.

Internet Addresses

**Over 100 Years Later, Black Cadet Gets His Due
(Reprinted From *USA Today* by the People's Weekly
World July 29, 1995, p. 5.)**

    <http://www.hartford-hwp.com/archives/45a/016.html>

United States Military Academy at West Point

    <http://www.usma.army.mil/>

**University of North Carolina at Chapel Hill Libraries:
Documenting the American South
The Colored Cadet at West Point: Autobiography of
Lieutenant Henry Ossian Flipper.**

    <http://docsouth.unc.edu/flipper/menu.html>

Index